The Complete
Book of
Dollmaking

WATSON-GUPTILL ✂ CRAFTS

The Complete Book of Dollmaking

A PRACTICAL STEP-BY-STEP GUIDE TO MORE THAN 50

TRADITIONAL AND CONTEMPORARY TECHNIQUES

PAMELA PEAKE

WATSON-GUPTILL PUBLICATIONS NEW YORK

A QUARTO BOOK

Copyright © 1997 Quarto Inc.

First published in the United States in 1997 by
Watson-Guptill Publications, a division of
BPI Communications, Inc., 1515 Broadway, New York,
NY 10036

Cataloging-in-publication data is available from the
Library of Congress

ISBN 0–8230–0773–1

This book was designed and produced by Quarto
Publishing plc, The Old Brewery, 6 Blundell Street,
London N7 9BH

Senior Editor: Gerrie Purcell
Editor: Maggi McCormick
Senior Art Editors: Catherine Shearman, Penny Cobb
Designer: Siân Keogh
Photography: Richard Gleed, Anna Hodgson
Illustrators: Terry Evans, Elsa Godfrey, Kate Simunek,
Dave Kemp
Picture researcher: Zoë Holtermann
Editorial Director: Pippa Rubinstein
Art Director: Moira Clinch

Printed in China

Typeset by Central Southern Typesetting, Eastbourne,
Great Britain
Manufactured by United Graphics (pte) Ltd, in Singapore
Printed by Star Standard Industries (pte) Ltd, Singapore

First printing, 1997
1 2 3 4 5 6 7 8 9 / 05 04 03 02 01 00 99 98 97

Publisher's Note

Contents

MAKING A START: BASICS AND TECHNIQUES

BASICS	8–29
Equipment	8
Coloring tools	10
Body fabrics	12
Dressmaking fabrics and trims	14
Stuffing materials and methods	16
Patterns and layouts	18
making a pattern	18
Needles, threads, and stitches	20
Wigmaking materials and tools	22
Modeling tools and materials	24
Kits and manufactured components	26
Accessories	28
safety considerations	29

TECHNIQUES	30–89
Proportions	30
Articulation	32
soft dolls	32
wooden dolls	35
composition and all-bisque bodies	35
Faces	36
drawing and coloring faces	38
face transfers	40
setting fixed eyes	41
embroidered faces	42

wax dipping	42
painting faces	43

Hair — 44
styling hair	46
styling hair for small dolls	49

Dressmaking — 52

Needle sculpture — 56
techniques for making a needle-sculpted head	58

Face masks — 60

Armatures — 64

Molds and press molds — 68
making a quick-impression mold	69
making a one-part plaster mold	70

Paper and papier-mâché — 72
papier-mâché	73

Working with wood — 76
spoon heads	78
clothespin (peg) dolls	79

Modeling — 82

Modeling basic heads and limbs — 84

Sculpting a character doll — 86

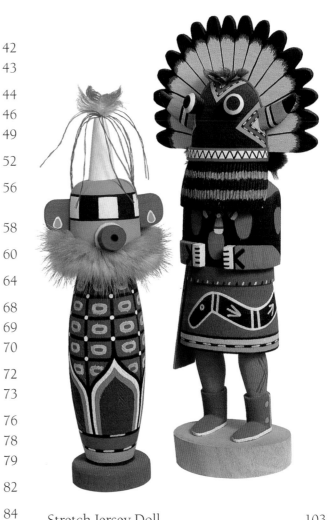

DOLLS TO MAKE

Simple starter dolls — 92
triangular pillow doll	93
making the rectangular pillow doll	94

Basic Cloth Doll — 95

Crafted Cloth Doll: Lavinia — 98

Stretch Jersey Doll	103
Felt Doll	106
Spoon Doll	111
Baby Dolls: Sleepy Heads	114
Armature Doll: Hannah	116
Poseable Character Doll: Santa Claus	119
Dolls' House Doll: Emma	125

CUTTING GUIDES AND PATTERNS — 128–141

Index	142
Credits	144

Making a start:
basics and techniques

The *Basics* section in this chapter acts as an introduction to the tools and materials used for dollmaking. The section includes information on preparation of patterns and fabrics and provides all the basics needed for getting started. The *Techniques* section that follows describes how to work with different materials from sewing to sculpting and then how to draw and paint appealing faces.

equipment

DOLLMAKERS USE A WIDE VARIETY OF MATERIALS
TO CONSTRUCT THEIR DOLLS, SO THERE IS AN EQUALLY
WIDE VARIETY OF TOOLS INVOLVED. HOWEVER, ALL THE
BASIC TASKS OF PATTERN MAKING, CUTTING, AND SEWING
USE DRAWING AND SEWING EQUIPMENT READILY FOUND IN
MOST HOMES. INDEED, WITH LITTLE MORE THAN FABRIC, SCISSORS,
NEEDLE, THREAD, AND A HANDFUL OF STUFFING, YOU HAVE ALL THAT
IS NECESSARY TO MAKE A START WITH FASHIONING A CLOTH DOLL.

As you work through the book developing and
extending your skills, you will be introduced to new
techniques that sometimes require more specialized
equipment. These new items for your workbox will help
you achieve the best results possible for each task and
give your dolls a more professional finish.

If you are just beginning, then start with the essential
equipment outlined here. It covers the items that will be
used most frequently.

GENERAL DOLLMAKING EQUIPMENT
Scissors (1) A selection of sharp scissors is essential:
dressmaking shears for cutting fabrics; pinking shears for
trimming raw edges; small, sharp-pointed scissors for
embroidery; and finally a medium-sized all-purpose pair
for general hand sewing.
Measures (2) Tape measures and a yardstick (meter
rule) for measuring fabrics.
Basting thread (3) For basting (tacking).

Strong thread (3) Buttonhole twist and quilting thread are suitable for attaching heads and limbs.

Embroidery threads (3) Six-stranded embroidery floss (cotton) for sewing features.

Sewing threads (3) A selection of cotton, silk, and polyester threads suitable for both hand and machine sewing.

Needles (4) Sharps for general sewing and hand-sewn seams; darners for needle sculpture and reaching awkward spots; ballpoint needles for sewing knitted fabrics by hand (they are blunt ended, so do not catch or split fibers of the material); bodkin for threading elastic and ribbons; dollmaking needles or long thin darners for joining limbs; and crewel needles for embroidery.

Seam ripper (5) For removing seams.

Pins (6) Glass-headed pins are best for general work as they are easily accounted for; long thin rustless Bridal pins, for working with delicate fabrics.

Cloth markers (7) Tailor's chalk, water-erasable marking pen, iron-on transfer pencil, lead pencils HB and 2B, and fade-away marking pens.

Thimble (8) To protect thumbs and fingers from needles.

Junior saw (9) For simple woodwork.

Craft knife (10) and cutting board To protect work surfaces.

Pliers and wire cutters (11) For bending, twisting, and cutting wires and pipe cleaners.

Fabric eraser To remove lead pencil marks from fabric.

Pencil sharpener To keep all marking pencils sharp.

Steam iron Suitable for pressing a variety of fabrics.

Embroidery hoop or frame For sewing features.

Glue and adhesive White craft glue (tacky glue) that can be thinned with water, dries clear, and is flexible. This essential, all-purpose glue has many uses in dollmaking. Fabric glue stick is a water-soluble basting adhesive taking the place of basting stitches. Fray Check commercial edge sealer prevents fraying of seam edges, dries clear, and can withstand washing. Woodworker's white craft glue (PVA) for working with wood.

Stuffing sticks Chopsticks and lengths of doweling.

Surgical forceps and hemostats Hemostats are artery forceps that lock tight when closed. Use them to catch seams when turning fabrics inside out and to hold elastic taut when stringing dolls (see p.35).

Sandpaper Various grades for sanding wood, papier-mâché, and painted surfaces.

Sewing machine With a selection of needles to sew both delicate and heavier fabrics.

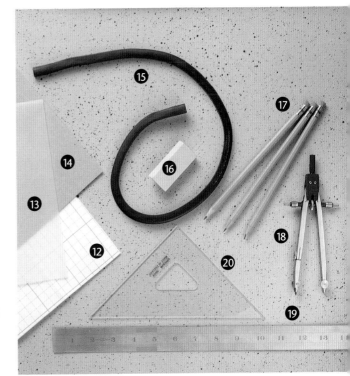

EQUIPMENT FOR MAKING PATTERNS AND TEMPLATES

Dressmaker's graph paper (12) These ready-prepared grids are usually ruled with 2 in (5cm) squares. To adapt one for use with the doll patterns, you will have to draw in intermediary lines to make 1 in (25mm) squares. Use a contrasting colored fine-line pen to make squares stand out more clearly.

Tracing paper (13) For use with a master grid and for tracing full-size patterns.

Cardboard (14) Thin cardboard for making full-size patterns and templates. If you draw around cardboard patterns, you don't need to use pins as you would with paper patterns. Also, they last longer than paper patterns if you plan to make the same doll more than once.

Flexicurve (15) For drawing long curves more easily.

Eraser (16) To erase pencil and chalk marks.

Pencils (17) Both medium-hard and soft (HB and 2B).

Compass (18) To draw exact circles and semi-circles where necessary.

Rulers (19) Long and short rulers: 12 in (30cm) and 24 in (60cm).

Set square (20) To draw exact angles.

Paper scissors For cutting paper and cardboard.

Paper glue To attach pattern pieces together where necessary.

Pencil sharpener To keep marking pencils sharp.

coloring tools

THERE ARE MANY DIFFERENT MATERIALS SUITED FOR OUTLINING
AND COLORING FEATURES AND HIGHLIGHTING COSTUME DETAIL.
PENS, PENCILS, AND CRAYONS ARE EASY TO USE AND
REQUIRE NO OTHER EQUIPMENT TO OPERATE THEM. YOU
WILL NEED TISSUES TO WIPE NIBS CLEAN AND A
SHARPENER OR KNIFE TO KEEP A GOOD POINT ON THE
TIPS OF THE PENCILS AND CRAYONS.

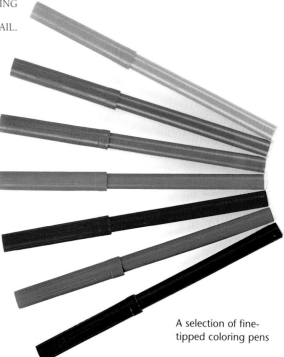

A selection of fine-
tipped coloring pens

PENS, PENCILS, AND CRAYONS

Pens are soft-tipped, with either fine fiber or broad felt
tips, and the inks may be water-soluble or permanent
when dry. Some need heat treatment with an iron to fix
them and make the color permanent. Choose those
where the color is permanent and will not bleed, fade, or
smear when dry. Colors for these pens tend to be bold
and harsh with no subtle shades, and the most useful for
faces will be black, brown, red, blue, and green. New
varieties of pens are constantly appearing, and all are
worth investigating and experimenting with, particularly
the Micron Pigma .01 waterproof pens. Look for them in
arts and crafts supply stores as well as quilt shops and
the larger stationery suppliers.

Before using any pen, test it on a scrap of fabric to
see whether bleeding occurs. If it does, prime the surface
with clear fabric sealer.

Fine-tipped pens are best suited for outlines and fine
detailed lines because they are easy to control. Broad-
tipped pens such as T-shirt markers are often too bright
for faces and are better reserved for coloring other
features such as clothing, shoes, or hair.

Colored pencils have softer colors and produce more
delicate hues, especially if you use the side rather than
the tip. Use crayons the same way to avoid a waxy look.
Use both for shading and blushing. Some crayons need
heat setting with an iron to fix the color. Follow the pack
instructions.

BRUSH-ON COSMETICS

Dry blusher can be used on fabric to color cheeks, knees,
and elbows, while eye shadow can be successfully used
to shade eyes. The color is not permanent, and will fade
over time. However, this is easily overcome by applying
more blusher every so often or by spraying with acrylic
sealer to set the color permanently.

PAINTS AND PAINTING EQUIPMENT

Oil-based paints have generally been replaced by acrylics,
poster paints, and the new water-based enamels. China
paints, which can be both oil- and water-based, are used
specifically for painting porcelain dolls and have a special
technique of their own, as well as a need to be kiln-fired
at 1330°F (720°C). For this reason, they lie outside the
scope of this book. Acrylics are the most popular of the
other paints because of their versatility. They can be used
on many different surfaces and dry quickly, and brushes
can simply be cleaned in water. When dry, acrylics are
both hard and water-resistant.

Acrylics are available worldwide, with variations
specially formulated to work on specific surfaces such as
wood, fabric, papier-mâché, and ceramics. These
preparations are generally sold in a fluid form, and the
colors may be somewhat limited compared to the choices
offered to artists in tubes of pure pigment. Choose
whichever product you feel comfortable with, as the end

results will be similar. When using the pigment, you may need to prepare the surface with a sealer or primer. You must thin the pigment with water to make a wash or add medium to increase the flow, opaqueness, or gloss. Finally, acrylics can be sealed with brush-on or spray fixatives which are clear and either matte or gloss.

Useful colors to have in your paintbox include the following pigments: titanium white, permanent yellow, black, raw sienna, Hooker's green, cadmium red deep, ultramarine blue, Venetian red, cadmium yellow light, cobalt blue, burnt umber, pale olive green, and cerulean blue.

Water-based enamels are highly glossed craft paints suitable for all surfaces, wood and paper in particular. They dry relatively fast, and are fadeproof, hard, and water-resistant after 24 hours. White enamel makes wonderful bright highlights to eyes and can be applied in minute amounts on the tip of a fine sewing needle. Again, brushes are easily cleaned in water.

Finally, there are a few other brush-on items that should not be overlooked. Clear nail polish (varnish), is a readily available sealer that adds brightness to eyes, while small drops, skillfully applied, make very good tears. Glitter paints and glitter glues can be used as eye shadow and on cheeks to add sparkle. The base is colorless when it dries, so only the glitter specks remain to be seen. Finally, typist's correction fluid, also known as liquid paper, is a source of a good bright white paint. It is especially useful for painting the whites of the eyes on a dark fabric if you don't have a collection of regular paints.

EQUIPMENT FOR PAINTING

Brushes (1) Ranging from a very fine 6/0 for detail work through to larger sizes for applying base coats and all-over skin tones.

Palette or a glazed white tile (2) For mixing pigments.

Paints (3) Either in tubes or jars.

Palette knife (4) For mixing colors.

Paint tray For mixing liquid paint.

Water jar To mix with watercolor paints.

Tissues To clean up brushes.

Cocktail sticks For stirring small amounts of paint.

Small sewing needle For applying eye highlights.

Crow-quill pen or map pen To draw fine lines.

Sponge To apply paint.

Textile medium To convert any acrylic paint into a non-bleeding fabric paint.

Retardant To slow down the drying time of acrylics.

Acrylic gesso A white primer and sealer for wood, papier-mâché, and other non-oily surfaces.

Acrylic clear matte sealer To seal the color and make it washable.

body fabrics

GENERALLY THE MOST SUCCESSFUL BODY FABRICS ARE THOSE THAT HAVE A GOOD FIRM WEAVE, IN A COLOR AND WEIGHT APPROPRIATE FOR THE DOLL BEING MADE. IN ADDITION, FABRICS NEED TO BE NON-FRAYING, NOT TOO DIFFICULT TO TURN RIGHT SIDE OUT, AND OF SUFFICIENT OPAQUENESS TO HIDE THE STUFFING. THESE FABRICS ARE SHAPED INTO THREE-DIMENSIONAL BODIES BY THE CUT OF THE PATTERN, POSITION OF DARTS, AND TO A LESSER EXTENT BY THE PROCESS OF STUFFING.

Unbleached muslin (calico) has long been the preferred fabric for making traditional cloth dolls where both the body and the head require a firm weave. The deadness of the color can be offset by blushing those areas of "skin" that remain visible. When a doll has head and limbs made from polymer clays or similar substances, the color of the body fabric will be immaterial because it will be hidden by clothing. However, the fabric will certainly need to be heavy and firm enough to support the head and limbs. Muslin (calico) addresses all these issues and remains as much a dollmaker's favorite today as it always has been.

Other pure cotton fabrics that are suitable for bodies and heads are poplin, lawn, broadcloth, flannelette (winceyette), and Viyella, which is a fine brushed-cotton. Many of these are available in realistic flesh tones. Gone are the days when the nearest to flesh was a choice between vivid pink or a very dark brown. Quilt shops now stock a vast selection of solid-colored fabrics which include many hues of brown, beige, peach, pinks, ivory, ecru, tan, and black, all of which are sold year round. These shops are an alternative source to department stores, where the range tends to be both more limited and seasonal.

Problems that you might encounter will generally be wrong weight but right color, or right weight with the wrong color, both of which are relatively easy to overcome. Underweight fabrics can be used double or have strength added by applying an appropriate iron-on backing, while bright colors can often be dulled simply by soaking them in a bleach solution and then washing. Another option is to use a commercial dye and prepare your own color.

Cotton body fabrics

THE ANTIQUE LOOK

Many dollmakers wish their dolls to look old, to become instant heirlooms without the hassle of looking for genuine antique fabrics. An ingenious method that achieves just this is to dye muslin (calico) in a tea solution made by adding multiples of 4 tea bags to 20 ounces (600ml) of boiling water and allowing the mixture to steep for 15 minutes. The tea bags are removed, and prewashed fabric is soaked in the solution for about 20 minutes with occasional stirring to ensure even coverage. Remove fabric, rinse (optional), and then tumble dry to set the color. Keep dyeing until you have the desired color, then iron and make your doll.

In some instances, fabrics with different properties will be needed to meet design requirements. A body may need a fabric with a certain amount of give or stretch so shaping can be achieved by judicious stuffing rather than by pattern cutting and darts. Dolls with face masks as formers need a fabric that can be stretched and molded over the mask as it is glued in place, while dolls with needle-sculpted features will generally require a fabric with even more stretch.

Felt body fabrics

Stretch body fabrics

Felt is a nonwoven fabric available in several realistic skin colors. It has a pleasant texture, doesn't fray, and has a moderate degree of stretch. Select a good-quality felt with a high wool content; otherwise, it could split during stuffing. Weak felt tears easily; if necessary, reinforce it with a backing. Make sure that you use a stretch backing to complement the stretch of the felt.

Knitted fabrics such as cotton stockinettes, Swiss tricots, velours, jerseys, and double-knit synthetics (including the popular American brands of Windsor Ponte and Comfort) offer varying degrees of stretch. They have revolutionized dollmaking, opening up opportunities to create very innovative cloth dolls that are limited in their conception only by the skill of the maker.

Ideally, the surface of knit fabrics should be smooth rather than heavily ridged, fadeproof, have a soft pleasant texture, and, more importantly, a high degree of run resistance. The stretch may lie in one of two directions or in both directions on the same fabric. When the stretch lies across the fabric from selvage to selvage or around the tube, the resulting doll will be cuddly and plump, while a stretch that lies along the length of the fabric parallel to the selvage will result in an excessively elongated doll. Fabrics with stretch in both directions are best reserved for needle sculpture.

All knit fabrics should be tested to find the percentage of stretch before a doll is made, or undesirable variation from the design specification can result. Pull the fabric this way and that to determine its character, then make adjustments and cut accordingly.

THE STRETCH TEST

Mark a length of 10 in (25cm) on your fabric with pins at each end. Now hold the marked area against a ruler, stretch, and measure the new distance between the pins. Repeat the test along the grain of the fabric. Calculate the percentage by subtracting 10 from the stretched length in inches and multiplying the remainder by 10. Thus a fabric that stretches to 13 in (33cm) has a percentage stretch of 13 − 10 = 3 then 3 × 10 = 30%.

Patterns for the cloth-bodied dolls and fabric heads in the *Dolls to Make* section have all been designed for specific fabrics, and the best results will be obtained by using the fabric listed or a near equivalent.

dressmaking fabrics and trims

CHOOSING THE FABRICS AND TRIMS WITH WHICH TO DRESS YOUR DOLL SHOULD BE THE RESULT OF MANY DECISIONS. EACH COSTUME OR OUTFIT IS A CAREFUL BALANCE OF STYLE, WEIGHT OF FABRIC, CHOICE OF COLOR, SIZE OF PRINT, AND METHOD OF CONSTRUCTION. IT SHOULD COMPLEMENT THE DOLL, MAKING A PLEASING WHOLE. THIS CAN BE A BEWILDERING STAGE, BUT BY FOLLOWING SIMPLE GUIDELINES, YOU CAN ELIMINATE MANY PROBLEMS BEFORE YOU START.

FABRICS

The majority of projects call for modern fabrics that are readily available, and you should try to keep to the natural fibers: cotton, silk, and lightweight wool. Natural fibers are easy to handle, will gather and drape realistically, and hold pressed pleats and folds in place. Wool can be steam-pressed on curves to shrink it into place, while pressing also shapes bias strips, ensuring that they lie flat and smooth—little points, but very important when you are working on small garments.

Useful cotton fabrics are gauze (muslin), batiste, voile, lawn, organdy, poplin, sateen, satin, flannelette (winceyette), and velveteen. Silk dressmaking fabrics include brocade, crepe, georgette, net, organza, shantung, taffeta, and tussore. Wools present a problem because of their weight, but if you choose carefully and avoid designs with gathers, all should be well. Useful wool fabrics are fine cashmere, flannel, serge, velvet, and tweed.

Plain and patterned fabrics can both be used for clothes, and both features should be relevant to the period and style that you have chosen. Keep colors pale and subtle if you are in doubt. Bright, heavy colors can easily overwhelm a doll. Color should be authentic for old dolls. Aniline dyes were slowly being introduced in the last quarter of the nineteenth century, so, before that time, magentas, fuchsias, and certain greens and blues

Checked and plain dressmaking fabrics

would not have been possible. Consider dyeing your own fabrics, and remember to put trimmings and buttons into the dye bath to get everything coordinated.

Checks, stripes, plaids, and dots should all be suitably scaled, and their use is governed by the same factors that apply to full-size dressmaking, including extra fabric to match patterns. If you can't find a suitable print or pattern, consider making your own. You can embroider a simple design or enhance a basic print with embroidery stitches, draw with fabric pens and paints, or use stencils and stamps.

Dressing dolls' house dolls presents more challenges of scale. Fabrics must be truly lightweight, and prints, stripes, and checks smaller still. Silk is very good, especially if all raw edges are sealed and garments are hand sewn, while silk ribbons become skirts with no hemming needed.

Ribbons for trimming

Ribbons Available in such an array and produced in virtually every color possible, ribbons make wonderful trimmings. They offer an inexpensive way of adding excitement to an otherwise plain outfit. From narrow to wide, patterned or plain, ready-pleated or ruffled, soft or stiff, and even wired, there is a ribbon for every occasion. The more familiar ribbons are silk, satin, grosgrain, velvet, cotton, and polyester. Silk is the best choice, for it is soft, drapes well, and can be gathered without looking bulky. Nylon and other synthetic ribbons are not a good choice because they are crisp and tend to stick out. The colors also tend to be a little more harsh and bright.

TRIMS

Lace, ribbons, braids, cords, buttons, fringes, beads, and embroidery all play their part in finishing off an outfit and should be carefully selected using the same criteria as above. Scale is ever important, and if you are in any doubt, leave it off. Consider using a same-fabric trim instead made from the costume fabric and thus immediately sympathetic to the outfit. The options range from narrow tucks through frills and pleats to casual and fully fashioned tailor's bows. In some instances, the reverse side of the fabric can be used, opening up even more possibilities.

Lace has been used to decorate costumes since the sixteenth century. Handmade lace, whether worked by needle, bobbins, or pins, has always been treasured for its exquisite delicacy; indeed, it has long enjoyed royal patronage. Costumes for men and women at the European courts of old were covered in exotic lace creations, some worked in gold and silver threads. With the advent of machine-made lace, this trim became affordable by all, and there was a period in the nineteenth century when lace was used to decorate almost everything—and certainly every edge—in sight. Nowadays, lace for dollmakers tends to be reserved for trimming historically accurate costumes or for edging modern-day dolly underwear and special outfits such as christening gowns and bridal clothes. Choose lace carefully, paying extra for good-quality cotton and silk edgings. Remember that the design of some lace lends itself to being cut into narrower trims, while insertion lace can be joined together to make a fabric.

Braids and cords These are heavier trimmings altogether, and are more in keeping for use on coats, jackets, outerwear, and hats, where the fabric is also of a heavier weight. Russia braid is narrow and very good on doll clothes, and it can be split apart to make a narrow cord which is useful for making frog fastenings and piping. Rickrack, as we know it, is generally too big and heavy, not the same as that used in the nineteenth century. However, some Scandinavian countries still produce a very narrow rickrack to decorate their national costumes, and it is worth looking out for. Cords that you twist and plait using threads of your own choice are more in scale.

Patterned and printed dressmaking fabrics

stuffing materials and methods

A stuffed doll's body

THERE IS CONSIDERABLE VARIATION IN THE MANY DIFFERENT TYPES OF MATERIALS THAT CAN BE USED TO STUFF AND FILL DOLLS. TRADITIONAL STUFFINGS HAVE INCLUDED SAWDUST, SHAVED WOOD KNOWN AS EXCELSIOR, OLD RAGS, DRIED MOSS, CRUSHED NUTS, FEATHERS, KAPOK, WOOL FIBERS, AND EVEN SHREDDED PAPER, TO NAME BUT A FEW.

Nowadays, emphasis is placed on safe, healthy, non-allergenic stuffings that can be washed if necessary and, more importantly, both enhance and complement the design. Even though stuffings are packed away out of sight inside the doll, a wrong choice of material or even a badly stuffed body with correct choice of material could well spoil the shape and appearance of a doll.

TYPES OF STUFFING

Polyester batting (wadding) (1) Another version of polyester in which the fibers are formed into sheets about ½ in (12mm) thick. These sheets can be pulled apart into thinner layers or cut as strips. Batting is also available where the fibers are bonded together in a sandwich to prevent shifting. Sheets of bonded polyester batting can be cut to shape with scissors and used to line skins, a useful feature when granules are being used as a filler.

Plastic granules (2) Known variously as body pellets, plastic rice, or beans, all of which refer to the size of the granules. This material makes an ideal filler when weight is required. It behaves like a liquid, constantly on the move, so as dolls are positioned to sit up or lie down by rearranging the limbs, the granules flow into position and secure the pose. In large dolls, the weight of the granules becomes very lifelike. This puts a strain on the seams, which will need to be double-stitched at least.

Pompoms (3) Small, fluffy yarn balls that are wonderful for contouring features such as cheeks, buttocks, and chins. They are simply positioned and held in place by stuffing from behind.

Pipe cleaners and chenille stems (4) Short lengths of wire with a soft covering. They are perfect for filling fingers in larger dolls and for making skeletons in smaller dolls. They can be used individually or together in pairs when more are needed to fill a space or to provide more strength, and they possess an additional bonus: they can be bent into shape.

Polyester fiber (5) A synthetic, soft, lightweight, bouncy stuffing that is probably the most popular choice. The fiber possesses a great number of desirable qualities. It handles easily, is clean and resilient to crushing (it readily springs back to a relaxed state), and is non-absorbent, which means that it washes well and dries quickly.

STUFFING THE DOLLS

Hardly any tools are needed for stuffing as most shapes stuff well by hand. Work consistently and patiently, turning the doll as you work, carefully observing the developing shape. Hold the skin firmly in your left hand as you stuff with your fingers closed on the seam line at the opening edge. Push each handful of stuffing well down with fingers or whatever stuffing rod that you have. Think of the body as a nest; push the stuffing to the outside walls and leave the central cavity till last. Use small pieces of stuffing for small areas and larger handfuls for bigger cavities.

Decide how firm the stuffing must be; a stretchy fabric will need a softer finish than a woven one. Mold the limbs and body with your hands, coaxing the stuffing into a pleasing arrangement. It might even be necessary to push a long darning needle through the body wall from the outside to arrange stuffing in a distant corner. If you are not happy, simply pull all the stuffing out and start again. It is the only remedy.

The work generally begins with extremities and tiny areas like fingers and feet. These are best turned right side out and dealt with before tackling the next part of the body. Twist a small piece of stuffing onto the tips of your forceps, then insert it into the fingers. Hold it in place from the outside with your other hand and gently withdraw the forceps, leaving the stuffing behind. Work back toward the opening, stitching any hinges as you come to them, and finally close the opening with ladder stitch (see page 21). When using granules, support the body well so that it will not tip over and spill beans everywhere. Use a funnel to guide the beans into position.

Another way to use beans is to wrap them in parcels of batting and insert as many parcels as necessary to fill the skin. These beans will provide weight, but not much more.

Batting strips are used rather like a bandage. Cut narrow strips for very small dolls and increasingly wider strips for larger dolls. Wrap them evenly around a body frame of wire or pipe cleaners; work up each arm and leg in turn, finishing with the torso. Add extra wraps over the buttocks and chest where more padding is required. A few stitches or a drop of glue will hold the ends in place. Bodies prepared in this way need not have an outer covering and can be dressed directly if the clothes are not going to be removable.

These general directions for stuffing are applicable for most dolls, but there are occasions when a more creative approach will be needed. It might be a combination of stuffings and techniques used together or a more innovative solution such as an amorphous bag of stuffing sculptured into shape by the careful placement of stitches. Each project will direct you to the correct procedure.

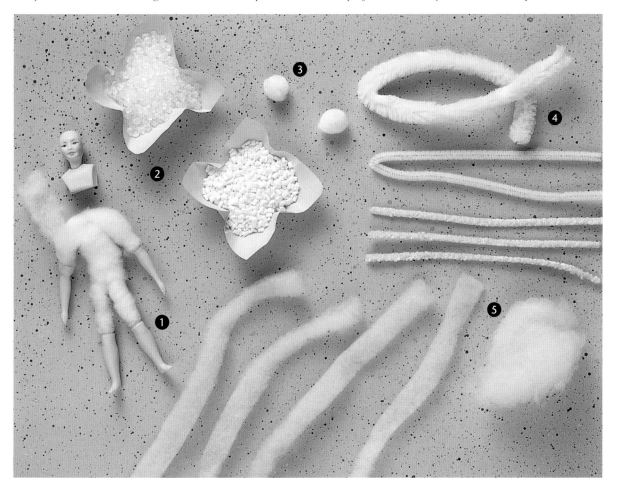

patterns and layouts

PATTERNS ARE THE MOST IMPORTANT PART OF ANY PROJECT, FOR
WITHOUT THEM YOU WILL NOT EVEN BE ABLE TO MAKE A START.
IT THEREFORE MAKES GOOD SENSE TO SPEND TIME MAKING AN
ACCURATE COPY AND GETTING TO UNDERSTAND ALL THE MARKINGS.

The patterns for the projects in the *Dolls to Make* section
have been presented in one of three ways. Those that are
simple shapes, such as rectangles for skirts and
petticoats, are given as measurements in the *Cutting
Guides.* You can either draw these directly onto the
wrong side of the fabric ready for cutting, or make a
paper pattern and proceed in the usual way. Second,
small dolls may have their patterns presented full size
because they fit comfortably within the page. In this
instance, you need only trace them directly from the
page in order to get a working copy.

Then there
are patterns that
have been
reduced in size
to fit on the page and
then overlaid with a grid of
squares. The size of the squares is
given in scale and will usually be 1 in
(25mm). In this instance, you will have to complete the
squares and enlarge the pattern to make a doll that fits
the measurements and material requirements.

MAKING A PATTERN

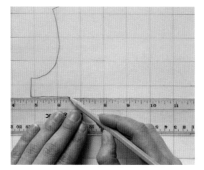

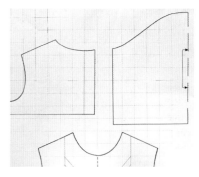

1. Make a reusable master grid by
drawing squares that match the scale
given onto a large sheet of paper.
Dressmaker's graph paper is a ready-
made alternative, but you will need to
draw 1-in (25mm) squares in a
different color to distinguish them
from the printed 2-in (5cm) squares.

2. Lay a sheet of tracing paper over the
master grid with the book nearby.
Transfer the outline of the pattern,
square by square. For some
symmetrical pattern pieces only one
half is shown with an instruction to
"place on the fold." To make it full size,
enlarge as directed, then cut out and
place on the fold of a doubled piece of
paper. Cut out, open it, and use.

3. Some pattern pieces have shared
outlines superimposed on top of one
another on the grid (body, front and
back, of Basic Cloth Doll, see page
131). Make separate patterns for each
piece along the correct outline.

On a photocopier you can increase
the percentage enlargement until the
squares reach the required size. Check
the size of the squares with a ruler.

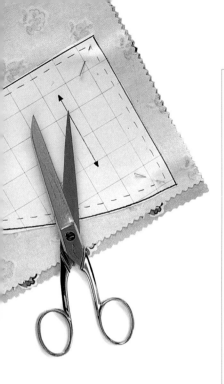

LAYOUTS

Prepare fabrics first by washing to remove any sizing (dressing), then iron to remove creases. Pull back into shape if necessary to make sure that the warp and weft are at right angles to each other. Add backings as required. Now lay folded fabric flat on a table with right sides together. Make sure you have all the pattern pieces needed for each fabric and lay them on the fabric, positioning first the longest and widest pieces, followed by the largest, down to the smaller pieces which can be used to fill up the spaces.

Paper patterns can be pinned onto the fabrics for cutting, or glued to cardboard and drawn around. Make sure you have distinguished between "cut two" and "cut a pair." There is a difference. Check that arrows lie parallel to the selvage. Note any special layout requirements for stretch fabrics. Also note clearly pieces that are sewn together before they are cut out. Finally, check your layout one last time, then make a sketch of it for future reference.

PATTERN MARKINGS

As each pattern is prepared, transfer information such as back, front, arrows, number of pieces to be cut, and so on, to the full-size copy. The following conventions have been used:

Grain arrow This indicates the straight grain, nap, pile, or knit direction of the fabric. Pattern pieces are generally laid on the fabric with the arrow lying parallel to the selvage. Felt does not have a grain; therefore, the pattern pieces will not be marked with an arrow.

Cutting line Cut on the inside of the cutting line; otherwise, your doll or the clothes will start to get bigger than intended.

Sewing line This is the line along which seams are sewn and darts are made.

Seam allowance This is the area between the cutting line and the sewing line. It will be ¼ in (6mm) unless otherwise stated.

Fold line This marks the center of a symmetrical pattern piece.

Guide line Used to mark a placement line for topstitching, gathering, or attaching hair, for example.

Match points Letters or bullets to clarify sewing sequences.

Centers Center front and center back.

Clip Clip seam allowance to release tension.

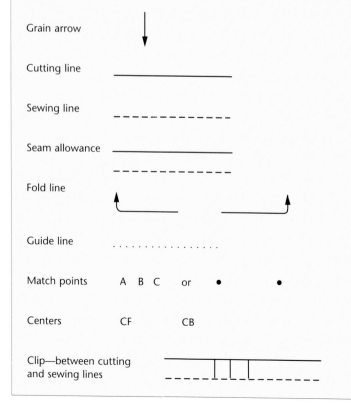

Symbols used for PATTERN MARKINGS

Grain arrow

Cutting line

Sewing line

Seam allowance

Fold line

Guide line

Match points   A B C   or   •   •

Centers   CF   CB

Clip—between cutting and sewing lines

needles, threads, and stitches

THE SEQUENCE OF SEWING CLOTH BODIES OR CLOTHES TOGETHER IS GIVEN IN DETAIL WITH EACH PROJECT, BUT IT IS IMPORTANT TO REALIZE THAT THERE ARE BASIC METHODS OF WORKING WHICH APPLY TO ALL.

Cotton and polyester threads

Fancy threads

Fine cotton-threads

Use the finest needles possible, whether sewing by hand or machine, so fabrics are not marked with holes, and the correct style of needle for specific tasks, such as sharps for seams, crewels for embroidery, betweens for quilting, and so on.

An all-purpose cotton-covered polyester thread is suitable for machine work and general sewing. It is versatile, easy to use with both synthetic and natural fabrics, strong and washable, and will not shrink (causing puckered seams). When dressmaking for dolls' house dolls and using very much finer fabrics, you will need even finer threads such as Mettler Stickgarn No. 60/2 or Gutermann No. 50, both of which are cotton, together with Nos. 10, 11, and 12 sharps for hand sewing.

SEAMS

A seam allowance of ¼ in (6mm) is included on all pattern pieces except where specifically mentioned otherwise. An extra allowance is provided for turning under, hems, and some gathering. Seams can be worked by hand or machine, although it is sometimes easier to sew small, intricate parts slowly and carefully by hand.

In most instances, the seam allowance can be judged by eye and checked with a seam gauge. Less experienced stitchers might prefer to mark the seam line with a fade-away pen or a colored basting (tacking) thread which can be removed. Another popular method for sewing accurate seams is to use a template. Make a cardboard copy of the pattern that stops at the seam line, draw around the template on the fabric, and

then sew along the line. This is a good method for sewing intricately shaped pieces.

When sewing by machine, corners and curves can be maneuvered by lowering the needle into the fabric, lifting the presser foot, and pivoting the fabric to the new direction. Then lower the presser foot and continue sewing. Use backstitch for hand sewing and a straight stitch on the machine, ensuring that seams for stuffed body parts are strong enough. Double-stitch if in doubt.

All flat seams should be pressed as they are made, while curved seams should be clipped or notched on inner and outer curves respectively, to reduce seam bulk when turned right side out. Corners should be trimmed by cutting away on the diagonal. (See diagram 15, right.)

FUNCTIONAL STITCHES

Stitches that you should be familiar with for general hand sewing are running stitch for basting and gathering, backstitch for seams, herringbone to close slashed openings when it is only necessary to bring the edges together (as in trapunto work), overcasting to whip edges together, stab stitch for topstitching when a row of sewing is worked on the right side, and ladder stitch for closing seams invisibly.

Ladder stitch, sometimes called blind stitching, is used to close seam openings on all body parts, attach heads to necks, and when "plastic surgery" is needed to hide sagging areas. It is no more than a hidden running stitch worked from the outside surface and when it is finished, it should be invisible. Always use a strong thread and work from right to left, finishing by backstitching along a seam before cutting the thread. Suitable threads are extra-strong hand quilting thread, linen upholstery threads, buttonhole twist, and mercerized tatting thread or crochet cotton.

DECORATIVE STITCHES

Embroidered facial features are worked with six-stranded floss (cotton). Any number of strands from one to six will be used, according to the scale of the feature being worked. Stitches most frequently used are stem stitch for outlines, satin stitch for solid blocks of color, French knots for freckles, straight stitch for eyelashes, and buttonhole stitch for irises, while velvet stitch, French knots, and bullion stitches all make good textural coverings simulating hair and curls when worked on the heads of small cloth dolls.

Traditional embroidery stitches used for decorating costumes are feather stitch, chain stitch, and fly stitch, as well as the stitches used for smocking. Other useful stitches such as raised chain band and Pekinese stitch can be used when purchased braids would be too heavy. At this point, gold and silk threads can be introduced, and you will find more information as well as instructions for working these fancy stitches and many more in most general embroidery books.

Glossary of STITCHES

FUNCTIONAL

1. Running stitch
2. Backstitch
3. Herringbone stitch
4. Stab stitch
5. Ladder stitch

DECORATIVE

6. Stem stitch
7. Satin stitch
8. Buttonhole stitch
9. French knot
10. Straight stitch
11. Bullion stitch
12. Feather stitch
13. Chain stitch
14. Fly stitch

SEAM

15. Clipping a seam and corners

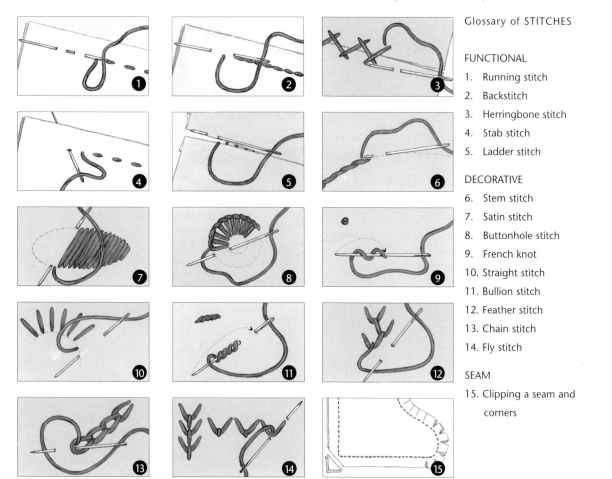

wigmaking materials and tools

Knitting yarn

HAIR CAN BE MADE FROM THE MOST AMAZING VARIETY OF FIBERS AND MATERIALS, RANGING FROM REALISTIC TO FANCIFUL. ANYTHING GOES, PROVIDED THE HAIR, STYLE OF DOLL, AND CLOTHING ARE ALL COMPATIBLE WITH THE CHARACTER BEING MADE. AFTER ALL, AN EXQUISITELY DRESSED PERIOD COSTUME DOLL WILL NOT BE RIGHT WITH STREAMERS OF BUBBLEWRAP PLASTIC, NOR WILL A RAG DOLL WITH A COIFFURE OF CLAY CURLS.

MATERIALS

Materials commonly used to make wigs include knitting yarn, mohair, jute, flax, hemp, string, bunka, embroidery thread, silk, real and fake fur, felt, ribbon, shredded fabric strips, and various synthetic fibers. Fibers, both natural and synthetic, are available in many forms, and dollmakers are really spoiled for choice.

Knitting and crochet yarns are available in a multitude of colors, plies, and textures that can be fine and smooth, thick and knobbly, wiry, or silky. They make excellent choices for wigging cloth dolls.

Mohair from the angora goat is one of the best fibers to use for realistic wigs. It is finer and less expensive than human hair, with a lovely soft texture and good sheen. It is a very satisfactory material to work with, as you can do almost everything with mohair that you can with real hair. It can be dyed, permed, and curled using hairdressing lotions and equipment. However, treat it carefully, and avoid washing it, for mohair can mat and shrink. Drycleaning is the answer.

Wefted mohair fl

Wefted processed mohair

Viscose or rayon

Crepe mohair

Mohair is available in several forms. First, there is the fleece, known as staples, in which the fibers are left just as they are when sheared from the goat; they are sold unwashed or washed and wefted. A weft is a row of hair stitched along one edge to give some strength, and so it is ready to be applied directly to the head or wig cap. Then there are skeins of mohair in which the fibers have been cleaned, dyed, and combed, and then processed into continuous lengths. They are not spun into a yarn, so strictly speaking these are hanks or skeins of rovings. Always look for skeins that have long staples of about 12 in (30cm), which will mean buying the best grade possible as used in the making of wigs for the theater. Cheaper mohair is of an inferior grade made from short underhairs, not worth considering for wigmaking.

It can also be bought as crepe mohair woven between a pair of strings. This is ready to use immediately by simply removing the strings and gently teasing the fibers apart before attaching it to the head. It is ideal for the smaller-sized cabinet dolls and dolls' house dolls.

WIG CAPS AND PATES

Some wigs can be worked directly onto the head of a doll, while others may need to be constructed on a base, which could be either a wig cap or pate. Different materials can be used for making these caps. The choice depends on the fiber being used, the style of the wig, and whether it will be glued or stitched together. Familiar examples are of stretchy nets held snugly in place with elastic along the hairline, cloth caps with darts for shaping, and buckram that has been dampened, stretched, and then molded to fit the head.

Wig caps Dolls' house dolls are too small for conventional fabric wig caps and need a much thinner alternative. Plastic food wrap is ideal for making these caps.

Pates Pates are cork, rigid cardboard, or stiffened fabric domes glued over the openings of hollow heads. They cover and shape the crown and can be used as anchors for wigs.

TOOLS

Essential tools for wigmaking are few and simple. Apart from white glue and sewing equipment, you will need home hairdressing equipment such as hairdriers, curlers, brushes, and combs.

Additional items that are useful for making these small wigs are a soft baby's toothbrush and a metal dog comb with evenly sized and spaced teeth.

For making curls and ringlets, you will need a selection of different-sized rods. These could range from lengths of dowel as thick as your little finger to barbecue skewers and even finer cocktail sticks or a set of knitting needles and fine sewing needles for very thin curls.

Yarn styles often need to be wound around templates, and while books and large pieces of cardboard will suffice, you may like to invest in specially designed hair looms.

Knitting needles

Buckram

Wooden skewers

Hair loom for winding yarn

modeling tools and materials

SCULPTURED DOLLS ARE SHAPED BY EITHER CARVING AND CUTTING AWAY FROM A BLOCK OF MATERIAL OR BY BUILDING UP, LAYER UPON LAYER, WITH A MODELING COMPOUND. THERE ARE NO PATTERNS TO FOLLOW. THIS IS A CASE OF WORKING ALONG WELL-ESTABLISHED GUIDELINES BASED ON AN UNDERSTANDING OF BODY PROPORTIONS AND FOLLOWING YOUR OWN INCLINATIONS. IT IS A SKILL THAT CAN BE LEARNED. PRACTICE AND EXPERIMENT WITH DIFFERENT MODELING MATERIALS. THE RESULT WILL BE AN INDIVIDUAL PIECE OF WORK, AN ORIGINAL THAT CAN GIVE ENORMOUS SATISFACTION.

Sculpting tools

MATERIALS

Any material that you can mold is worth considering, and those that are readily available or easily prepared at home are a good place to start. They should all meet the basic requirements of being able to hold a shape, set hard, be lightweight, and be strong. Once dried or cured, you should be able to work on your model, refining details before painting.

Dough and papier-mâché Various homemade doughs and papier-mâché mash fulfill these requirements and are inexpensive to produce. They are natural materials mixed with white craft glue (PVA) or cellulose glues and fillers, and generally can be stored without fear of drying out, but they must be kept covered until you are ready to use them. Being organic materials, they need a preservative added to their composition; otherwise, bacteria, and even mice or insects, can attack and destroy your work. Sawdust is another product that can be mixed with glue and water to make a modeling paste, but unlike those mentioned above it has to be used immediately.

Milliput This two-part epoxy putty is the favorite modeling material with many miniaturists. It can be formed, and, when it is set, it can be worked on to refine details. Unlike other materials, this really is unbreakable.

Plastic wood Sold by the building trade for repairing cracks, nail holes, and chips in wood, can be used like putty and built up in thin layers to make simple models.

Modeling clay (Plasticine) This is an oil-based clay that never sets. It is an intermediate modeling material for

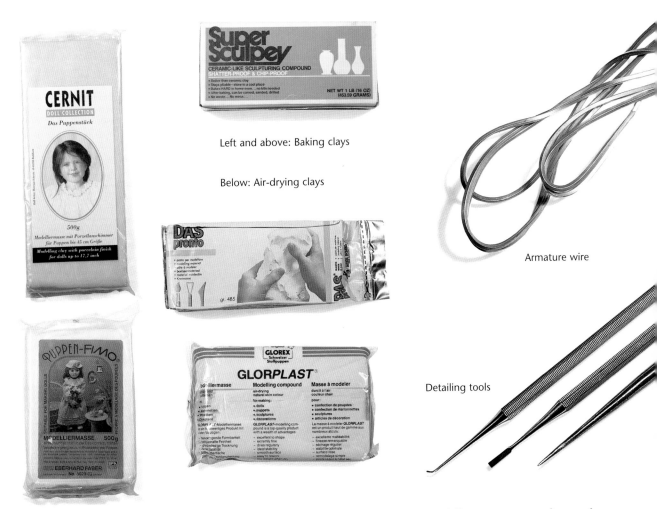

Left and above: Baking clays

Below: Air-drying clays

Armature wire

Detailing tools

many different processes. It can be used to create detailed sculptures from which molds and press molds are made, or as a former to be covered with a thin layer of plastic wood or papier-mâché—or even cloth—to make face masks or whole heads. Once the covering material has set, the clay can be removed and used again.

Clays New developments with clays have resulted in products for dollmakers that are considerably cheaper and easier to use than natural clays. Based on polymers, they are divided into two distinct types. One group is air-drying, while the other needs to be cured at low temperatures in a household oven.

There are many brands of both clays. Consult local doll studio or craft suppliers to find what is currently available. Some brand names for air-drying clays are Daz, Creative Paperclay, Celluclay, La Doll, and Glorplast. All are easy to use and can be sanded, filed, and carved once they are dry. The more popular bakeable clays are sold under the brand names of Fimo, Puppen Fimo, Cernit, and Super Sculpey. They all behave in a similar way even though there are subtle differences. Fimo is often used for very small dolls and accessories, while Cernit creates surfaces that resemble porcelain with a wax finish. However, it is expensive, so it is often used over a foundation of Super Sculpey.

TOOLS

Modeling is very much a hands-on process, where your fingers do a lot of the work, assisted by a few basic tools. Start by working on a large glazed tile that can be raised to eye level and rotated so that the work can be viewed from all sides; heads can be shaped on the necks of tall weighted bottles. Special turntables can be purchased when you need them.

Most tools can be improvised when you are starting. Use needles for drawing on clay, spoon bowls and handles for smoothing, craft knives for cutting and carving, and dental tools for adding small pieces and detailing the clay. If you enjoy modeling, consider investing in a set of ready-made tools.

kits and manufactured components

Armature skeleton

THERE IS A BEWILDERING ARRAY OF COMMERCIALLY AVAILABLE ITEMS ASSOCIATED WITH DOLLS. THESE PRODUCTS RANGE FROM SEPARATE ITEMS LIKE JOINTS, EYES, HEAD FORMERS, WIGS, AND SKELETONS TO KITS THAT CONTAIN EVERYTHING NEEDED TO MAKE A SPECIFIC DOLL. TRYING TO FIND WHAT IS AVAILABLE AND WHERE IT IS, AND THEN WHETHER THE SIZE OR COLOR WILL MATCH YOUR NEEDS CAN BE DAUNTING. START WITH CRAFT CATALOGS AND LOCAL DOLL STUDIOS, FOR THEY WILL HOLD STOCKS OF MORE COMMONLY USED EXTRAS AND CAN DIRECT YOU TO THE LOCATION OF MORE ELUSIVE ITEMS.

BODY PARTS

The following list outlines many of the commercially made extras that can be purchased:

Eyes of every color and size are made from inexpensive flat acrylics to individually matched pairs of handblown glass with threaded irises, expensive but extremely realistic and very desirable. All are for fixed settings in dolls with hollow heads and for incorporating in clay models. You can also buy mechanisms to go with stalked glass eyes that allow them to open and close. Then there are sheets of painted eyes for gluing onto hard heads and appliqué eyes for sewing onto cloth.

Wigs, like eyes, are available in a wide variety of sizes and colors, as well as being made from a choice of different fibers and in so many styles. Acrylic wigs are affordable, but tend to be brash when used on reproduction antique dolls. Human hair and mohair, although more expensive, offer a more realistic alternative.

Eyelashes are sold as matched pairs and in long strips that can be cut to size. Remember that false eyelashes sold at the cosmetic counter for people can also be used on dolls simply by trimming them to size. Save small end pieces for smaller dolls.

Limbs showing the components in place

Head former

Joints allow a body to move at the hips, shoulders, and neck. Rotational disk joints that snap together by hand are now made in white plastic so they don't show through the body skin and have largely replaced the traditional wooden joints with split pins that are popular with toymakers. There are also some ingenious neck joints that allow the head both to rotate and to nod up and down. They are made for cloth dolls but unfortunately are not always easy to find. Porcelain dolls incorporate many joints in their bodies; these are always worth adapting for use in other materials if possible.

Face masks are either cheap plastic, brightly painted, and ready for immediate use, or of a higher quality sold either covered with cloth and painted, not painted, or simply a clear molded shape left for you to cover in fabric of your choice and then paint.

Head formers are usually made of Styrofoam (polystyrene) and made to fit behind a matching mask. Consider using them as a base with air-drying clays and other modeling compounds.

Bodies are available in all sizes and with all degrees of articulation, from fully jointed composition to more rigid, stuffed cloth. However, most are made for use with porcelain heads or for joining to porcelain limbs, so they may not be helpful for dollmakers working with other materials.

Armatures and skeletons are either metal plates that can be bent to shape in specific areas of the body or plastic snap-lock systems that extend from limb to limb in a continuous unit via the backbone. Other components that are available are teeth, tongues, head and neck domes, individual limbs, finished and part-finished heads, hooks and elastic for stringing, face transfers, and body skins ready for stuffing.

Kits

Kits provide everything or nearly everything you need to make a doll. They are both mass-produced by manufacturers, and made in smaller numbers and even limited editions by individual doll artists, so there is a wide variety and quality to choose from. For many, this option will not even be considered because it detracts from the pleasure of making a doll in its entirety. However, before you dismiss the idea, consider the following advantages:

- It provides one-stop buying, since everything is provided.
- It provides an opportunity to experience working with different materials without having to invest in new and possibly costly equipment.
- It could be a way of learning new techniques.
- It allows you to make cheaply a doll that would otherwise be too expensive to buy.

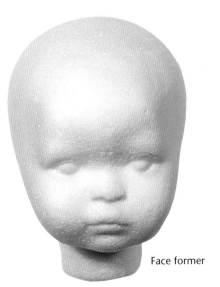

Face former

Face mask

accessories

THE BODY IS COMPLETED, AND THE DOLL IS NOW READY FOR THE FINAL STAGES. THESE WILL START WITH DRESSING, FOLLOWED BY THE ADDITION OF ALL THOSE EXTRAS THAT BRING YOUR DOLL TO LIFE AND GIVE IT THE CHARACTER YOU ARE SEEKING, AND LASTLY, PRESENTATION. SOME PEOPLE BUY READY-MADE OUTFITS, CONSIDERING THEM FAR SUPERIOR TO ANYTHING THEY COULD EVER HOPE TO MAKE, WHILE OTHERS WILL PURCHASE A PAIR OF LEATHER BOOTS, SOME SOCKS, A STRAW BONNET, OR SIMPLY A PAIR OF GLASSES FOR A GRANNY WITH FAILING EYESIGHT.

Many of us will have a box full of items like small bears, musical units, or jewelry waiting for an opportunity to use them. Finding accessories for dolls of different sizes and styles is not easy, so it makes sense to hoard treasures in advance. It is easier to find items for dolls' house dolls, since there is so much available at a standard scale of $\frac{1}{12}$th.

Marvelous examples of the use of accessories are provided by English "peddler" dolls with their trays full to overflowing with special items, costume dolls complete with trunks of clothes, and baby dolls with entire layettes. Use your Santa Claus to display a whole host of toys bursting forth from his sack.

Of course, a play doll will be moved from situation to situation and the child will improvise accessories when they are needed.

However, other dolls will have to sit, stand, or be propped up. They need to be displayed, and while doll stands are an easy choice, they can be sterile and spoil the arrangement and line of a costume. Consider making a wooden base that can be varnished, painted, or covered with velvet. Then figure out how to pass support rods from the base into the doll. Using doll furniture is another possibility. Having achieved a pleasing position for the doll, it then becomes a case of what can it hold, or what can be put beside it, to create an interesting arrangement.

Adding accessories is both challenging and fun, and for most dollmakers, it becomes an opportunity to indulge in a little play as the scene is being set. The thought and effort you put into displaying your doll will be amply rewarded with praise from those who see it.

English Peddler, designed by Lesl Roberts and interpreted by Sylvia Critcher, with a wonderfu array of accessor displayed on her tray.

SAFETY CONSIDERATIONS

Safety issues fall into two major groups. First are those concerned with the suitability of a doll as a play item for a young child; the other is centered on good workshop practice that covers your own safety when making any kind of doll.

Protecting children at play is often a matter of applying common sense and making sure that the doll is suitable for the child for whom it is intended. All materials used should be new, clean, flameproof and non-allergenic, and should meet safety regulations currently in force. There should be no small parts that could be detached and swallowed nor anything sharp, while granular fillings must be enclosed inside a strong bag that is separate from the doll skin.

The second issue of concern centers around yourself, the tools and materials you work with, and how you organize your work space. There is an area of potential danger here that is easy to forget, but due care and an advance knowledge of the materials being used will minimize these and make sure that safety is paramount.

Always work in a clean, well-lit, and well-ventilated room. Keep electrical tools in good repair, with cords (flexes) behind and under work surfaces, never exposed in areas where you walk.

SAFETY POINTS

• Have a specific place to store everything so that tools are kept together and not left lying around, especially those with points, sharp edges, and cutting surfaces.

• Keep reagents, glues, fixatives, paints, and media on a shelf or in a cupboard away from light, heat, and children. Always check safety labels and be aware of potential dangers in advance so that you are prepared for any contingencies and know the course of action to take in case of mishaps.

• Some materials may be new to you. Always read instructions carefully and follow them explicitly. This is especially true when working with the new clays, either air-drying or low temperature curing. When used correctly they are not hazardous.

• Polymer clays leach plasticizer if they are stored too long, and this destroys plastic and furniture, so be careful how and where you store them. For some, the dust from sanding may be an irritant and you may need barrier creams, gloves, masks, or goggles for protection. Some clays, when overheated, give off toxic gases, so follow instructions carefully. Check your oven performance with a thermometer and never leave pieces unattended while curing.

• Also be aware that Styrofoam, which is a trademark for polystyrene foam, should never be used as a former under a clay that requires baking in an oven because when it is heated it gives off deadly gases.

proportions

BEING ABLE TO MAKE A WELL-BALANCED DOLL WHERE LIMBS, TORSO, AND HEAD HAVE PLEASING PROPORTIONS IS THE AIM OF ALL DOLLMAKERS. IN PEOPLE, THESE PROPORTIONS ARE CONSTANTLY CHANGING FROM BIRTH THROUGH CHILDHOOD TO MATURITY AND BEYOND, AND ALTHOUGH IT IS NOT NECESSARY FOR DOLLS TO BE REALISTIC IN PROPORTION, THEY STILL HAVE TO CONFORM WITHIN REASON.

Emily by American doll artist, Diana Effner, reproduced and costumed by Sylvia Critcher.

By understanding this principle, you will be able to design dolls representing specific age groups, determine sizes of body parts to go with heads, and make corrections to patterns that leave something to be desired.

Dollmakers follow artists' rules of proportion, in which all measurements are based on the size of the head. Thus an adult male has a body height eight times the length of his head, which is measured from chin to upper forehead, while a mature woman is described as being 7½ heads tall. A newborn infant, however, is proportionately half this size, with a head measuring one-quarter of its entire length. The height for different age groups is tabulated below, together with examples for two different sizes of heads.

During growth, the relationship of the length of the head to the length of the body changes, as do the arm and leg proportions. A baby's head will fit twice into its body, the bend of the legs disguises their true length, and there is no well-defined neck, hands, or feet. A two-year-old also has a head that fits twice into the body length, but the legs are longer. At birth, the navel is in the lower half of the body; between eighteen months to two years, it is exactly halfway, and from then on, it is in the upper half of the torso.

Young children are about 11 years old before their arms are long enough to reach over their head to touch the opposite ear. At this age, girls have the beginnings of a waist and signs of puberty, and by 15 the halfway point of the body is the crotch. For boys, this is when shoulders broaden and a more typical masculine physique begins to appear. Thus the hip line gradually becomes the halfway point, and by maturity elbows are level with the waist, wrists are level with the crotch, and outstretched arms, measured from fingertip to fingertip, equal the total height.

AGE IN YEARS	0–1	2	4	7	ADULT FEMALE	ADULT MALE
Height expressed as the number of times the head fits into the body	4	4½	5¼	6	7½	8
Total height when head length is: 1½" (36mm)	6" (15cm)	6¾" (17cm)	7⅞" (20cm)	9" (23cm)	11¼" (28.5cm)	12" (30.5cm)
Total height when head length is: 2½" (6.5cm)	10" (25cm)	11¼" (28.5cm)	13⅛" (33cm)	15" (38cm)	18¾" (47.5cm)	20" (51cm)

WORKING IT ALL OUT

When designing a doll or sculpting a head, you need to know what size to make the limbs and torso for the doll to be correctly proportioned. For some, this will be an intuitive process, but others will have to figure it out using the chart. The measurements given here are a guide only.

(**Right**) Lay the head and any other body parts on a sheet of paper with appropriate measurements ruled alongside to correspond with the selected age. In this way you will be able to plan a body for your doll that has the correct proportions.

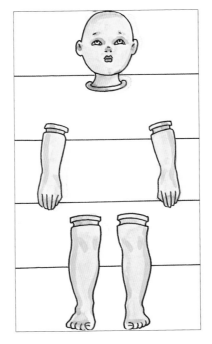

HANDS AND FEET

(**Below**) Hands are very expressive and by their gestures can contribute enormously to the character of a doll. Generally they are the same length as chin to forehead, and the middle finger is as long as the palm. Outstretched fingers will easily cover the face—try it with your own hand to get a feel of the size. Feet, on the other hand, tend to be ignored and hidden away in shoes. An adult foot is on average as long as the face, but, like hands, will look better on a doll if it is made slightly smaller.

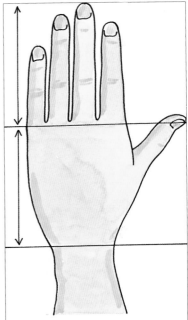

HEADS

(**Below**) A head alters shape during growth as much as any other part of the body. For an infant, whose bone structure has yet to develop, the face is round with a small nose and mouth and undeveloped chin, and all facial features lie in the lower half of the face. By six years of age, the nose is becoming longer and narrower, the jaw develops as the teeth appear, and the eyebrows are above the halfway line. An adult head has the eyes lying halfway, and there are clearly marked male and female differences in proportions. These are highlighted in techniques for drawing and painting facial features.

articulation

ATTEMPTS AT REPRODUCING JUST SOME OF THE MANY COMPLEXITIES OF
HUMAN MOVEMENT IN DOLLS HAS LONG CHALLENGED BOTH THE
IMAGINATION AND SKILL OF DOLL ARTISTS, AS MOVING LIMBS AND HEADS
THAT CAN BE POSED UNDOUBTEDLY ADD GREATLY TO THE APPEAL AND PLAY
VALUE OF DOLLS.

All manner of ingenious methods and devices for
articulation were developed during the heyday of dollmaking, with the introduction of new and exciting
materials in the nineteenth century. Hollow-bodied
composition and ceramic dolls could be given limbs
articulated by a system of cleverly designed interlocking
joints, all held together by elastic or springs, while other
innovative methods of movement ranged from the
highly intricate wind-up clockwork mechanisms of
automata to gussets in leather-bodied dolls. Indeed,
most of the popular jointing techniques currently in use
today are a direct result of developments from this
period.

The choice of jointing methods that can be used in
any one particular doll are largely determined by the
nature of the materials used to make the doll. A soft doll
with a head and body made from cloth will generally
need different joints from a cloth-bodied doll with a
hard head and limbs or hard dolls which in turn may be
either solid or hollow. The following techniques are a
selection of those most likely to be useful.

SOFT DOLLS

Very effective methods for providing
movement in these dolls can be achieved
quite simply by sewing and without the
need for any specialized equipment.
Joints range from robust stitched
hinges for the limbs
of play dolls to
disks that allow
various parts of the
body to turn in a
more natural way.

*Irebokuro, a strikingly
decorated cloth-bodied
doll by Sylvia
Critcher, with
innovative
articulation for
puppetry.*

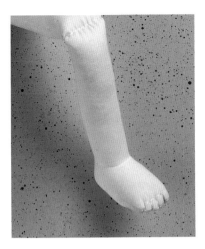

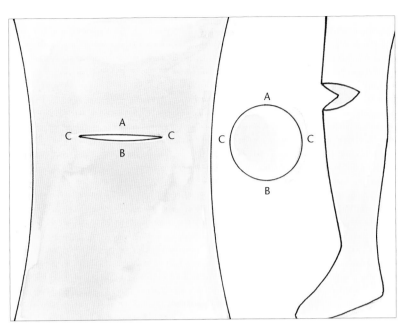

HINGES (Above) A hinge is a joint made by working one or two rows of stitching across an unstuffed portion of a limb, which allows the limb to swing back and forth or up and down. It is a floppy kind of joint, wonderful for play dolls where it is used to make hips, knees, and elbows.

As it is a flat joint, it is not particularly attractive to look at, a defect that is usually covered by clothing. Some solutions for making this type of joint more attractive, especially at the knees, are to decorate them with buttons or slide on big macramé beads.

GUSSETS (Above) A gusset is a small oval of leather set in a slash or seam of leather-bodied dolls. The resulting joint works like a hinge, but with one significant difference: the limb bends in one direction only and the movement is thus more realistic. The same technique can be used with cloth dolls if the raw edges of the slash are first bonded with interfacing.

SIMPLE PIVOT JOINTS (Below) These joints enable limbs to rotate fully and are used at shoulders and hips. The simplest method involves passing a strong thread through limbs and body from side to side and returning to the starting point, generally under an arm and tying off. It is a technique best suited for very small dolls, as are snap fasteners (press studs), which also provide a rather novel joint.

BALL-AND-SOCKET JOINT This is a three-dimensional joint and two different methods for making it have been used in the construction of Lavinia (page 98). The shoulder is a simple version with limited rotation. Here the socket is made by pushing in the side of the body wall to form a cavity for the naturally rounded ball end of the arm. The elements are then held together by a few strong stitches between the top of the shoulder and the arm.

KNEE JOINTS (Right) The knee joint is more complex and is achieved by pattern cutting and shaping with darts. The lower leg has a ball-shaped top that fits inside the socket of the upper leg. The elements of this joint work by pivoting on the threads which pass from side to side while the front edge of the socket prevents the knee from flexing forward unnaturally.

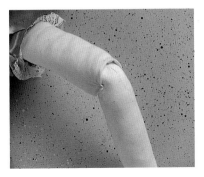

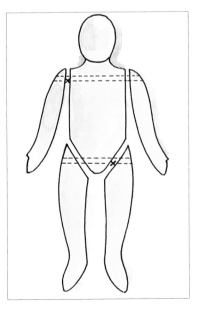

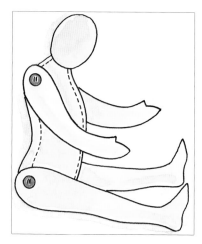

(**Left**) Larger dolls can be jointed by sewing through as described in Simple Pivot Joints on page 33, providing a needle can be passed through the limbs and body. These dolls usually have buttons to reinforce the turn on the arms, which enterprising dollmakers hide inside the limbs. In this instance the threads are passed back and forth through the body and the buttons in the limbs before the limbs are fully stuffed and closed.

INTERNAL JOINTS Most internal joint systems operate on a similar layered principle. Where the head and limbs join the body the two layers of fabric are sandwiched between circular disks which rotate on a central pin. Tension is governed by the tightness with which the disks are held together, which in turn controls the effectiveness of movement and poseability that is possible.

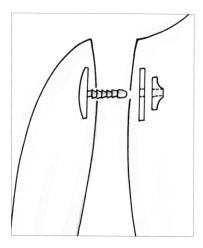

PLASTIC JOINTS (Above) These are a more recent development and are considerably easier to use. Each joint has three components: a disk with the "pin" molded on one side, a matching disk, and a locking washer.

limbs are on the right side before jointing with thumbs facing forward. Now place the remaining disk on the pin, then secure with the washer. Locking washers hold well enough when assembled by finger pressure, but the tension can generally be improved by placing a spool over the pin and tapping it firmly with a hammer.

WOODEN JOINTS WITH SPLIT PINS (Above) This is the traditional joint for both soft dolls and teddy bears. Each joint consists of two wooden disks, two steel washers, and a split or cotter pin. In addition, you will need a pair of long-nosed pliers to lock the joint in position.

1. Start by placing a washer on the pin followed by a disk. Now pierce the doll fabric with an awl (bradawl) at the point indicated on the pattern for the joint and feed the pin through this hole. Finish stuffing the head or limb,

and close the opening. Make a hole in the body wall at the relevant joint position and feed the pin through. On the inside of the empty body, place the remaining wooden disk on the pin, followed by the washer; then spread the tails of the pin apart.

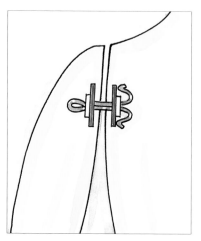

2. (Above) Press the disks together and hold firmly throughout the jointing procedure. Slide the tips of the pliers down the longest tail of the pin until they are ½ in (12mm) above the disk. Then pull up on the tail and bend it over so it forms a loop that sits on the disk. Repeat with the second tail.

(**Above**) Place the disk with the pin in the relevant limb or head, then finish stuffing as directed. Push the pin through the body wall and check that

WOODEN DOLLS

The mortise-and-tenon joints of early seventeenth-century English wooden dolls and the later Peg Woodens or Dutch Dolls span several hundred years and this attests to their popularity.

The peg doll on page 79 has a hole passing through the body. It lines up with the arms, which will articulate when they are strung together with a wire loop at each end, or elastic nylon fishing line knotted on each side. The attraction of nylon is that it can be melted into the holes by the heat of an iron. These same techniques can be used with any solid or hard-bodied doll.

(**Right**) Mortise-and-tenon joints are skillfully made joints requiring precision preparation and equipment which is beyond most dollmakers. However, while the thought of jointing wooden dolls may seem daunting to most, there are still several techniques for which you need not much more than a hand drill and saw.

(**Above**) Traditional wooden Amish dolls illustrate another technique, in which the legs and body are pinned together with a dowel. The movement results from the dowel fitting loosely into the legs so that they swing freely. It is not unlike the mortise-and-tenon joints of the Peg Wooden doll, which again are pinned together but all parts are closely fitted.

COMPOSITION AND ALL-BISQUE BODIES

(**Left**) These bodies are usually purchased already strung together with elastic. A simple body will have at least five parts, with articulated arms and legs at least, while other, more sophisticated bodies are designed with an incredible array of interlocking joints that provide all manner of ingenious systems for moving parts. While the methods for stringing them together are beyond the scope of this book, you should at least be aware of the basics, for the interchange of ideas among various methods of articulation will possibly provide a solution to a problem in the future.

faces

VIRTUALLY THE ENTIRE CHARACTER OF A DOLL CAN BE CONVEYED BY THE FACE, WHICH CAN EXPRESS ALL MANNER OF MOODS, FROM JOY TO DEEP DESPAIR, AND POINT TO AGE, SEX, ETHNICITY, AND WHETHER THE DOLL IS AWAKE OR ASLEEP.

It is certainly worth making a study of faces, for an appealing face can overcome almost any shortfall in construction or make a simple doll desirable. Conversely, a beautifully made and dressed doll can easily be ruined by poorly worked or wrongly placed features.

The position of the features on dolls with carved and modeled faces is highlighted by the contours, while the location of the features for flat-faced dolls are usually marked on a pattern or plan. Nonetheless, this aspect of dollmaking still seems to present problems. The techniques outlined here show first how to position the features and then how to decorate them with both traditional and modern methods.

POSITION OF FACIAL FEATURES

Positioning the features on a face, whether for an adult or child, follow fundamental guidelines based on proportions relative to age. These informal rules determine the position of eyes, ears, nose, and mouth and thereby eliminate guesswork. Babies generally have heads about 6 in (15cm) high, while an adult head measures approximately 9 in (23cm) and is thus a third larger. At birth, however, the head is a quarter of the total body height; for an adult it is one-eighth. Proportions alter considerably as children grow, accommodating the development of bone, cartilage, and teeth, which are all reflected in the position of features.

The eyes are the most important feature and getting them in the right place should mean that everything else will be in proportion. Practice drawing simple faces showing different ages on flat surfaces until you are able to draw them freehand with confidence without needing to erase marks or use a ruler. Then repeat the exercises on curved surfaces.

A selection of Chinese folk dolls with both embroidered and painted features.

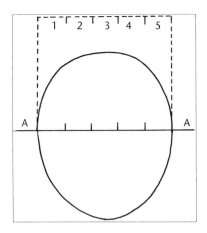

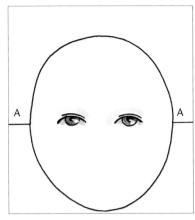

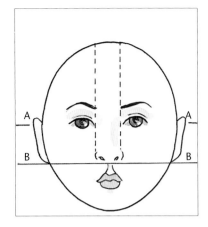

1. Starting with an adult head, draw an oval. Although there are variations between the sexes in general outline shape, this will not affect the overall effect. Divide the head in half horizontally, drawing a straight line from A to A. This line, which passes through the center of the eyes, can now be divided into five equal sections to determine the width of an eye.

2. Make a simple eye by combining the iris and pupil as a single black dot and position one in the middle of the second and fourth sections. The upper eyelid is more curved than the lower lid and will arch over the eye, covering the top of the iris—unless you particularly want a doll with a startled look. Eyes do not always need the lower lid, but eyebrows are essential.

3. Draw another horizontal line from B to B, halfway between A and the chin. This completes the two essential lines needed to finish placing the features. The nose lies within the central section of the face, between the eyes with the nostrils on Line B. The mouth and chin also lie in this central section, while the ears extend from a line level with the eyebrows down to B.

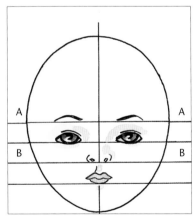

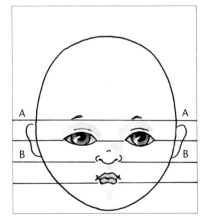

(**Above**) The halfway mark on the head of a child lies between the top of the eyes and the eyebrows, and is level with the top of the ears. Below this line the face can be divided into quarters, horizontally, with the eyes in the top quarter, the nose in the next, the mouth in the third, and the chin in the lower one. Boys and girls start to show differences in features from age of five.

(**Above**) Babies have a more rounded head shape, and the position of the features is markedly different. The eyebrows lie on the halfway line, so all facial detail is in the lower half of the head. The iris is nearly fully developed so less of the white is visible, making the eyes appear large; they are also spaced farther apart. The nostrils are halfway between eyebrows and chin.

DRAWING AND COLORING FACES

Fabric pens with permanent inks, colored pencils, and crayons can all be used to draw and color faces, producing effective, durable results.

PENS A variety of pens is available from art and craft stores, ranging from those with fine tips to broad-tipped T-shirt markers and others, more like stiff brushes. Pens with finer tips produce the thin lines needed for detailed work and outlining features. Prepare pens by shaking them and pressing the tip up and down on a scrap of fabric to check the ink flow. Test the ink to make sure it doesn't bleed into the surrounding fabric. Hold pens upright and use quickly and lightly. Hesitation may cause ink to spread off the line. Let each color dry before applying the next.

PENCILS Colored pencils and crayons offer many more subtle colors than pens and are therefore ideal for softer coloring of features and shading. Other options are glitter crayons for interesting sparkle effects, powder blush for cheeks, eyeshadow, and metallic glue pens that dry clear and leave gold or silver specks. Liquid paper, used for typing corrections, is ideal for eye highlights. Pencils and crayons need to be sharp and held upright for line

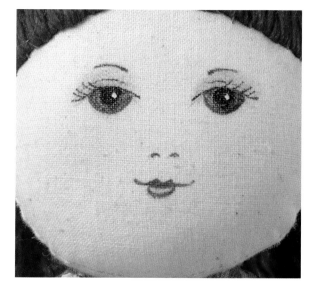

This basic cloth dolly has a simple but effective face in which the emphasis is placed on the eyes.

work, or held on their side for shading. Crayon color is usually fixed by heat sealing. Follow the manufacturer's directions. Alternatively, fix colors with a spray sealer.

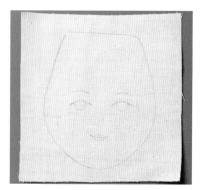

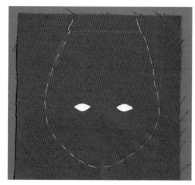

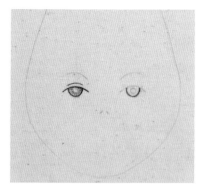

1. Copy the face from the pattern onto fabric using a soft lead pencil. Mark the essential details, not every feature, either freehand or by tracing, depending on your confidence. Include the head seam line so that the face can be centered. Any mistakes can be removed with a clean white plastic eraser.

2. When working on dark fabric, create the features using sharp chalk pencil. First color the bed of the eyes. Use a white T-shirt marker followed by liquid paper. Apply color from the outer corner of the eye toward the center; turn the face and work from the inner corner, covering the eye completely. Let it dry.

3. For the eyes, sketch a "U" for the iris with a fine-tipped blue or brown pen. Turn the face upside down. Draw short radial lines toward the center of the eye, leaving space between lines. Use a fine black pen to draw the upper eyelid and a smaller line behind for the eye socket.

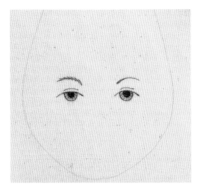

4. Color in the pupil and darken the outline of the iris to give a good clean edge. Two different styles of eyebrows are shown. Using a fine-tip brown pen, either draw a single line, thickening it at the inside edge, or draw a row of short, sloped strokes across the brow. In both instances, start at the inside edge and work out.

5. The simple eyebrow is completed with a red dot at the inside corner. The second eye has a lower eyelid, and the lashes match the feathered brow. To draw lashes, start with the pen on the line and quickly flick it out and off the fabric in a curve so the lashes don't end with little blobs. Test lashes on a scrap of fabric first. Draw in two nostrils.

6. To create the mouth, draw the center line with a fine-tip red pen, then color the lips with a red pencil. It is advisable to color sparingly, since more color can be added later. Note that the upper lip is darker than the lower lip.

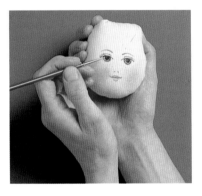

7. Carefully outline the upper and lower edges of the lips with a fine-tip red pen, then draw over the red center line with a fine-tip brown pen to take away the brightness of the color. Add more coloring to the lips, if required, especially the upper lip. The head should be sewn and stuffed before any more drawing and coloring takes place.

8. Bright eyes bring "life" to a doll's face. A single white dot on each eye will produce the desired effect. The white must be very strong; both liquid paper and water-soluble enamel work well. Use a thin brush or a fine sewing needle to put on a dot and repeat on the other eye, placing the spot in exactly the same position to avoid a cross-eyed doll.

9. Cheeks are shaded with red crayon. Take care to make soft edges. Alternatively, apply face powder with a cosmetic brush. Cheeks tend to fade and you will need to recolor now and again. Freckles add the finishing touch, created with fine-tip pen.

FACE TRANSFERS

Traditional transfer sheets for faces have been available since the late nineteenth century when they were intended as embroidery aids. Patterns for cloth dolls were often sold with several transfers so that choices of expression could be made and faces replaced as needed. Transfers are useful because the outlines of the features are automatically positioned and only need ironing to set them. These same transfers can also be used as guides for painted and drawn features.

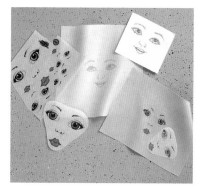

(**Left**) Recent advances have resulted in detailed full-color transfers for eyes and faces that can be used on fabric and wood. All are heat-bonded to the appropriate surface and a sealer such as clear nail polish, Mod Podge®, or Acrylic Gloss Medium and Varnish is applied to those used on stretch fabrics.

(**Below**) In addition, there are products available that make it possible to transfer color pictures to cloth. Essentially you make a color photocopy of your original and use it to prepare a transfer by covering it with a layer of bonding plastic that lifts the image and can then be applied to fabric. Using photographs of family and friends makes heirloom dolls with a difference.

SETTING FIXED EYES

Manufactured eyes, available in every size and color imaginable, range from inexpensive flat-backed acrylic eyes to more costly paperweights, which are handblown glass eyes of extraordinary beauty and quality. Most reproduction and many antique dolls have such eyes set in the head so they remain permanently open, in contrast to sleeping eyes, which are attached to rockers before they are set.

To set fixed eyes in a waterproof, hollow head, you will need the following items:
- Matching pair of eyes (flat or round backs)
- Small amount of sticky wax
- Plaster of Paris mixed to a dropping consistency
- Towel to rest the head on

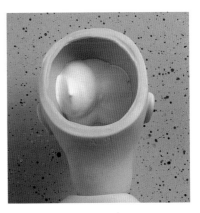

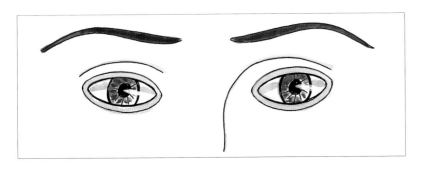

1. (Above) Roll wax between palms, forming a thin sausage. Place it in a ring on the front of the eye so it touches the edge of the eye socket. Position the eyes with pupils centered and level, then push each eye against the head so the wax sticks to the head. For a realistic effect, the top and bottom of each iris should be partly under the lids.

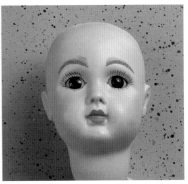

3. (Above) When both eyes are ready, lay the head face down on the towel for support and spoon plaster over the eyes. The plaster will puddle around them. When it has set hard against the porcelain, you can turn the head over and clean away excess wax with a warm, blunt tool.

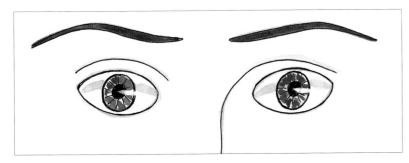

2. (Above) A more surprised or startled look is made by setting the eyes with a tiny bit of white showing above and below the iris, while a flirtatious glance is achieved by positioning eyes to one side.

Although these eyes are designed for nonporous heads, it is possible to first seal porous surfaces and then use plaster, or alternatively set with glue. Enterprising dollmakers have also used these eyes successfully in clay heads (Hannah, page 116), and with needle-modeled sculptures and face masks.

EMBROIDERED FACES

(**Above**) Embroidered faces for the Project Dolls have all been worked on finished, stuffed heads where the fabric is taut. Stem stitch is the most useful stitch; it can be used to "draw" faces and lines and to make solid blocks of color. Single straight stitches are useful for lashes and satin stitch for pupils. If in doubt about color, style, which stitch to use, or any other aspect of the embroidery, work a sample on spare fabric in a frame, which you should then keep for future reference.

For soft cloth dolls, embroidery has long been the favored method for making a face. The stitches needed are few and basic (see page 21) and the features are worked quite easily with needle and thread. Six-stranded embroidery thread should be separated into three or two strands for most faces and one strand for smaller faces and fine lines. For even smaller faces and more detailed work, use silk threads.

When selecting colors, choose one shade lighter than you think will be correct. For babies, keep the colors soft with pale rosy tints, and move to more definite colors as the age of the doll indicates. Avoid using black except for pupils; dark browns are better. Embroidery also works well with combinations of paint, pens, pencils, glitter glues, and cosmetic powder blush which can be used for cheeks and eye shadow.

WAX DIPPING

Coatings of wax soften painted features and give a dewy-skinned finish reminiscent of old-fashioned dolls. Materials suitable for dipping are those that hold their shape, such as composition, papier-mâché, wood, metal, and ceramics.

Prepare the head or limbs for dipping by devising a method for holding them safely. Chop equal quantities of beeswax and hard candle wax into small pieces and melt in a container that is deep and wide enough to accommodate the piece or pieces to be coated. This container must sit in a pot of water which is placed over low heat, and never left unattended. Test the wax with a thermometer; when it is 190°F (90°C), remove the container from the source of heat.

Dip the head into the wax and remove it in one continuous movement. Tilt the head so that the features are uppermost and excess wax can drain toward the back of the head. The wax may cloud, but will clear as it cools. If heads need a second dipping, reheat the wax and continue as before.

PAINTING FACES

Painting is probably the most satisfactory technique for creating highly individual faces, and by using pure pigments you will be able to mix colors and vary textures. Although there are paints formulated for working on different surfaces, water-based acrylics are the most versatile for dollmakers and will offer the most scope.

The colors most useful for your paint box are listed on page 11, together with the basic equipment needed to get started.

All surfaces to be painted need to be clean and free from grease and dust. In addition, some will need to be smoothed and primed, while others may need to be sealed to prevent paint from spreading or being absorbed.

WOOD Sand wood until it is smooth, working in the direction of the grain. Start with a medium-grit sandpaper and finish with a finer grit, wiping away sanding dust. In some instances you may need to seal the wood or prime the surface before painting. An alternative method for preparing wood is to use an acrylic gesso, which will give a smooth surface and prime the wood at the same time.

PAPIER-MÂCHÉ AND PLASTIC WOOD Use fine-grit sandpaper to remove any rough areas; then paint with acrylic gesso for a really smooth finish.

POLYMER CLAYS Providing that you smoothed the surface properly during modeling, there should be no preparation needed other than a light sanding and a wipe.

CLOTH Acrylic paint sticks to most fabrics without any bleeding, but to be on the safe side, test on the back of the head or on a scrap of fabric first. If you need to seal the cloth, use colorless medium where the paint is to be applied. A thinned-down solution of white craft glue mixed with water will achieve the same result. All sealers must be completely dry before you start to paint.

MIXING THE PAINTS Use a palette knife to mix pigments and always mix enough for the task at hand, making a note of the colors and proportions used. Mixing the paint with water makes it easier to work with and to spread as a wash. Adding acrylic medium will increase opacity. Paint should be applied in thin layers with adequate drying between applications to avoid peeling.

Flesh tones are needed on some surfaces before the features can be applied, and you will soon discover that there is no magic formula. Each doll and every surface is different and will have its own requirements. Experiment. Start with a good quantity of titanium white as a foundation, then add small amounts of burnt sienna and one of the reds for rosy flesh tones. A little extra yellow will lighten the tone and black darken it. A recipe for flesh to use with Super Sculpey can be found on pages 86–89.

The techniques used by artists for painting are extremely varied. Some prefer all brushwork; others incorporate pens, sponges, and pounces. Styles range from realistic portrait painting to more simple or stylized features. The position of the features, expressions, and any detailing required for painting is no different from that which has already been outlined for the other techniques. The advantage that painting has over other methods of coloring is the infinite variety of colors that can be prepared and subtleties of shading. Practice makes perfect in painting. Study the painting techniques used on old dolls of all kinds, as well as those used by modern doll artists.

Aurora, an original porcelain doll by Australian artist Maree Massey.

hair

HAIR IS THE CROWNING GLORY OF ANY DOLL, AND EACH WIG SHOULD COMPLEMENT THE AGE AND SEX DEPICTED AS WELL AS BE HISTORICALLY ACCURATE FOR A PERIOD DOLL. CURLED OR CROPPED, IN RINGLETS OR PONYTAIL, THERE ARE ENDLESS POSSIBILITIES FOR CREATING STYLES, AND THE TECHNIQUES USED WILL BE GOVERNED BY THE FIBER OR FABRIC CHOSEN FOR THE WIG.

When you plan a wig, always think it through carefully before starting. Consider the style required and the various elements like curls, braids, parts, and so on that will be needed in its construction, for this decision will govern your choice of fiber or fabric for the hair. Another consideration is whether some of the elements and hairpieces should be made in advance and then added to the wig as it is being constructed.

This, of course, means that you need to know how the wig is going to be attached to the head and whether the head needs any preparation. Will the wig be made directly on the head by gluing or stitching? If it is made away from the head, what sort of base will be used? All these questions and answers are closely linked and need to be considered as a whole.

Yarn hairstyle with braids, ringlets, and bun.

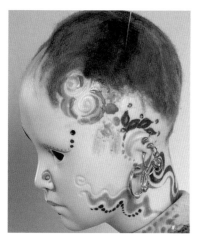

(**Left**) The projects illustrate how various popular fibers can be used, while the artists' dolls featured throughout the book provide a wealth of additional ideas that should prove informative and stimulating. Irebokuro, for instance, has a wig of handmade felt made from fine layers of commercially colored merino wool tops laid out in concentric circles in a star-shaped pattern to create an irregular edge. Boiled water has then been poured over the felt to mat the fibers together, and the whole wig has been supported on a shaped former and left to dry.

MAKING A BUCKRAM PATE

Dolls formed in a mold often have an open crown that must be covered. Such openings are usually below the natural level of the crown, so the head must be built up as well as covered. The following instructions for making a pate will achieve all this and in addition provide a hard skullcap on which the wig can be made.

1. (Left) Cover the head completely with two layers of plastic wrap (cling film) and fasten off around the neck by twisting or using rubber bands. Place some warm modeling clay (Plasticine) on top of the head, molding it to the required shape and thinning it down onto the doll to make a smooth seam. Cover both head and clay with another layer of plastic wrap.

2. (Above) Cut a square of milliner's buckram large enough to cover the head, and pass it through a solution of warm tea, which will both color and soften it. Place the buckram diagonally over the head, with corners at front and back and over the ears. Large heads may need a second layer of buckram for additional strength. Mold it on the head, spreading the fullness and pulling down to reduce wrinkles. Hold in place with rubber bands around the hairline.

3. Leave overnight to dry thoroughly, then remove it from the head and trim along the hairline, marking the center front on the inside of the pate with a pencil cross. Remove plastic wrap and clay from head and glue a piece of cardboard across the opening. The pate is now ready to use as a wig base and can be glued on the head when prepared.

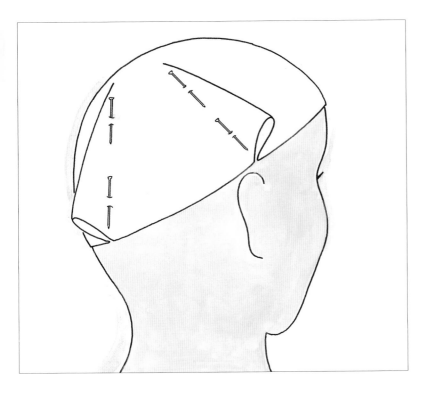

MAKING A SOFT WIG CAP

(Left) Many wigs are made by sewing wefted hair to a stretch net or fabric base. Cut a length of bias tape or wide elastic to fit around the hairline and sew it into a ring. Lay the net over the head, forming regularly spaced pleats on top of the hairline. Mark these darts with pins, then remove and sew. Finish the cap by sewing it to the band.

STYLING HAIR

There are several standard methods used to make basic wigs for larger dolls, and some styles may use any combination of these methods. Much will depend on whether the hair fiber is natural or synthetic, and whether it is to be pretreated before the wig is made. Natural fibers can be dyed with regular hair dye and curled as you would curl your own hair, using setting lotions, curlers, heated tongs, and so on.

Basic wigs are divided for convenience into the following categories: wigs made directly on the head of the doll; fabric wigs made by pattern cutting and sewing into caps; wigs made from strips of prestitched hair; and wigs made on a base that is then attached to the head. Try to be adventurous, read as much as possible, and be prepared to experiment. Use the following ideas to help develop techniques of your own.

(**Left**) Smaller curls can be made easily on wooden dowels and knitting needles, using a variety of sizes to match the size of the doll. Wind the fiber evenly around the "curler." Place the dowel in a tall container of hot water and remove to dry naturally or in an oven. Curls can be left as long ringlets or cut into smaller sections as required. This method of making curls in advance is easier than making curls on a finished wig.

WIGS MADE DIRECTLY ON THE HEAD (**Right**) can be either glued or stitched in place. They can be simple or complex as illustrated by Santa Claus, pages 119–124, where theatrical crepe has been glued directly onto a hard scalp and also used for eyelashes, mustache, and beard. Untreated crepe is a softly waved fiber, but when it is carefully steamed, the fibers straighten out, producing the very different effect illustrated here.

Embroidered hair is made directly on the head of fabric dolls, and you will find useful stitches on page 21. Yarn can also be sewn to a cloth head along part lines or around the hairline framing the face, simulating the growth pattern of real hair. It is then pulled together and styled, or glued and stitched down when it is left as straight hair.

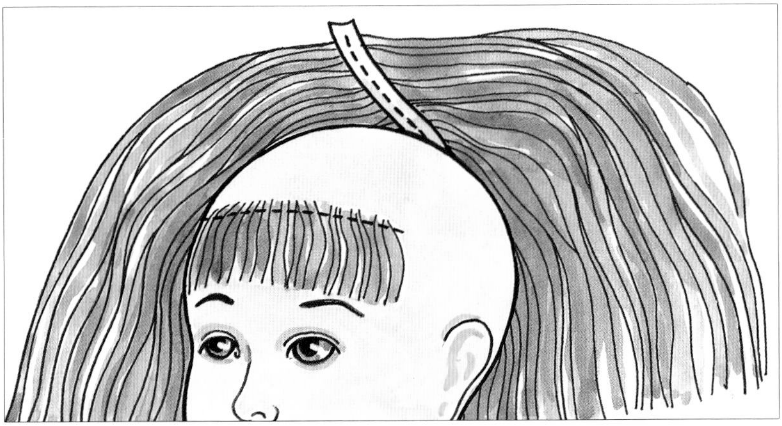

STRIP WIGS (Left) The simplest wig consists of a single strip that reaches from the front of the head to the crown with a part either in a central position or on the side. The strip can be backstitched to the head along the part or glued, while the remainder of the strip is either lightly glued to the head or caught down with a few stitches. The addition of a second strip or bangs across the forehead greatly extends the possibilities of this style.

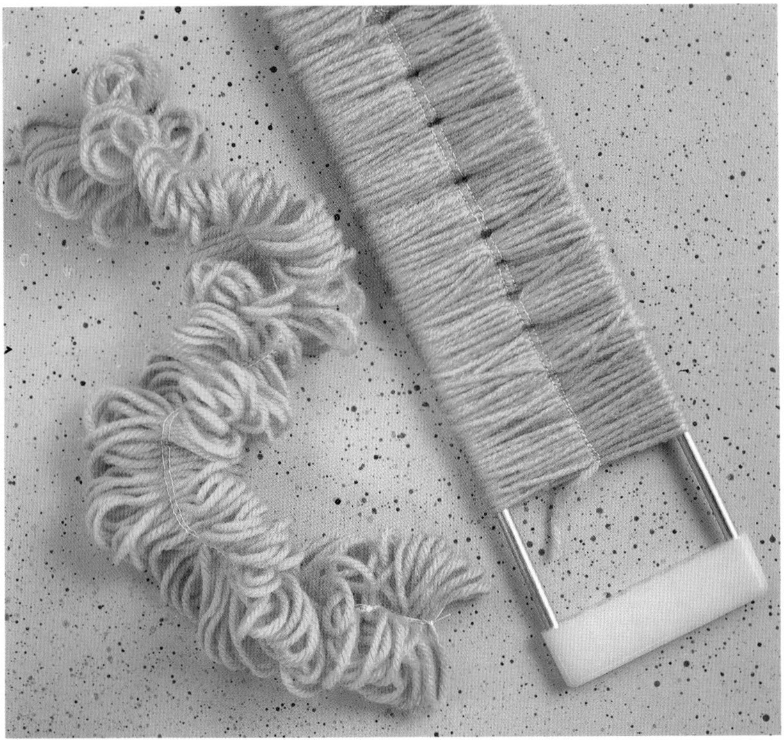

(Above) Yarn curls are made by winding yarn around a frame and stitching the loops through the center to make a strip that can be backstitched or glued to the head, working from the hairline back toward the crown. The loops can be left or cut as desired. A frame can be made from coathanger wire or a pair of needles threaded through wooden blocks.

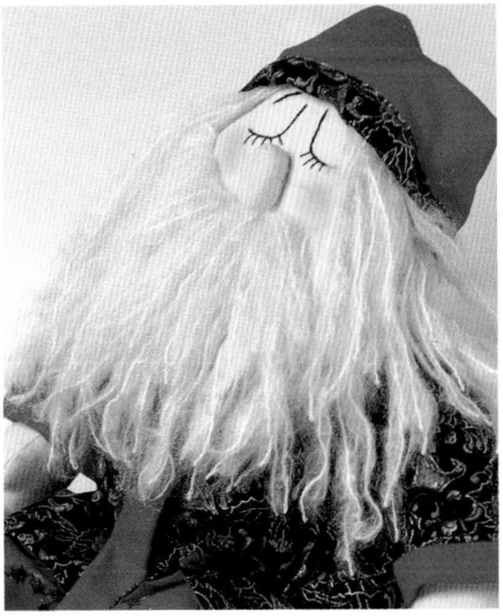

(Above) Sleepy Santa has a mohair yarn style consisting of two fringes of different lengths. The fringe for the beard is cut twice the length needed and stitched through the center to make a part that reaches across the front of the face. It is then backstitched to the face through the seam so that the upper half of the bangs falls down to conceal the part. The fringe for the hair is made in the same way but is longer and wider, reaching around the head from ear to ear.

WIGS MADE ON A BASE Most commercial wigs, both for dolls and people, are made by sewing strips of wefted hair to a net cap, a technique that can be used with buckram pates when gluing replaces stitching. Wefted hair can be purchased ready-made, unpicked from a full-size wig, made on a weaving frame, or more simply by sewing.

Reproduction Kestner "Oriental" doll with wig, which was made following the instructions below.

(**Right**) Spread a bunch of fiber out and line up the ends to make a wide band. Sew 1 in (2.5cm) in from the edge, then fold the short edge over and sew another seam close to the fold. The resulting weft is glued to a hard pate or stitched to a soft cap in a spiral pattern starting at the hairline and working toward the crown.

(**Left**) Wigs made in this way have a bald spot in the center that has to be covered with a topknot. First, make a small hole in the pate. Then tie a tuft of hair in the middle, fold it in half, and poke the fold down through the hole and glue it in place. A short length of weft can also be rolled to fit the hole and glued in place. Spread the tuft of the topknot open, cover with a damp cloth, and gently press flat with a cool iron. The J.D.K. "Oriental" lass has a wig made this way on a buckram pate using commercial black weft, while the style is a simple bob with bangs (fringe).

STYLING HAIR FOR SMALL DOLLS

Wigs for small dolls are usually made from either mohair or viscose fiber and less frequently from silk tops and fine sewing threads. Styles can be fashioned directly on the head, but a much preferred method is to make a thin wig cap from plastic wrap on which the hair can be styled and then conveniently removed while the doll is being costumed. This prevents unnecessary damage from overhandling.

Most small wigs consist of elements made in advance and then incorporated in a style. At this size, effect is more important than detail, and all cut ends and seams can be conveniently hidden by hairpieces, ribbons, and hats.

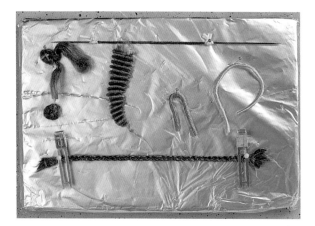

(**Above**) Preparation of curls, braids, and buns are all facilitated by using a plastic foam board covered with foil as a work station. Glue used to set hairpieces will not stick to foil, and various elements being prepared can be pinned to the board where they can be kept safe while drying or waiting their turn to be used.

"Mein Leibling", an all-bisque dolls' house doll with viscose wig in a style that complements her late nineteenth-century costume. This charming doll was made by the author and costumed by Sylvia Critcher.

CURLS AND RINGLETS Learning how to make small curls is essential. Used alone they can make quick and simple styles, while more elaborate curls are necessary for period hairstyles and coiffures.

Remove a strip of viscose from the hank by pulling it away from the side. Run this strip through water to dampen it; then carefully pull on one end, extending and drawing the strip out into a long, thin fiber. Move your fingers along the strip to a new position each time you have extended it to the required thickness. Practice drawing out until you can produce good long, thin fibers with a regular thickness.

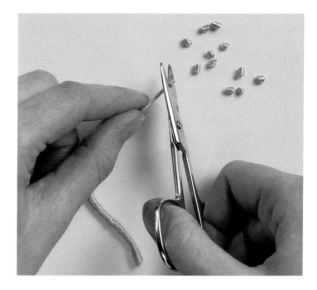

Viscose curls made on a knitting needle falling as a pony-tail.

(**Above**) Wind the fiber around a thin knitting needle—or rather hold the fiber still and turn the needle. The fiber can be fastened with wire twist ties at each end and then left to dry. Slide curls off the needle and cut into long lengths to make pairs of ringlets that are joined at the top or very short lengths for individual curls. Individual curls can be dropped onto a glued head to make a style that is suitable for most youngsters.

FLOCKING (**Above**) A fine downy hair suitable for babies, balding gentlemen, mustaches, and eyebrows can be made by cutting across the ends of a bunch of viscose with fine scissors so that the trimmings collect into a pile. Again, glue is spread on the head or relevant area, and the flock pile is dropped onto the glue, pinch by pinch. Leave it to dry and then blow or shake off the excess. If there is a bald spot, apply more glue and repeat the process.

BUNS Fashion a simple bun by tying a single knot in a length of viscose, or make a more elaborate one by tying several knots. Trim excess fiber, glue the ends under, pin it to the work board, and leave to dry. At some point during drying, lift and gently curve the back so it will dry shaped to the back of the head.

FOUNDATION WIGS (Below) The base for any small wig should be kept simple and serve as a foundation for attaching hairpieces. An effective start can be made by spreading glue over plastic wrap, winding a length of viscose around the hairline, then finishing it off at the back.

(**Above**) An alternative method for making a foundation wig is to run a line of glue along the hairline and then stick on lengths of fiber that can be pulled up and fastened off at the top, toward the back, when they are dry.

(**Right**) Make a center part for a foundation wig by running a line of glue from forehead to crown. Then carefully lay long fibers across the head. Rest a thin needle on the fiber above the glue, press down gently, hold it, then lift. This should leave an indentation. Pull the rest of the fiber gently toward the back of the head and glue down.

dressmaking

CLOTHES ARE AN IMPORTANT PART OF ANY CHARACTER, SETTING IT OFF JUST AS MUCH AS THE SHAPE AND FEATURES THAT MAKE UP THE BODY. WHETHER A DOLL IS FOR A CHILD TO PLAY WITH OR AN ARTISTIC EXPRESSION, THE COSTUME IS SUCH AN INTEGRAL PART OF ITS OVERALL APPEAL AND SUCCESS THAT CONSIDERABLE THOUGHT SHOULD BE GIVEN TO THE DESIGN AND CONSTRUCTION.

Reproduction Brevette Bru wearing a costume of shot damask silk, with plain silk for the hat and underskirt. Doll made and costumed by Sylvia Critcher.

Try to develop a total concept of the doll at the outset, as this governs age and gender as well as how it will be dressed and portrayed. Although decisions will have to be made along the way and ideas modified or changed, an end point is always in sight.

Decide whether clothes are to be removable, sewn in place permanently, or even built into the construction of the body, for this will affect the way they are constructed. Then consider whether the clothes are to be modern or reflect some historical period. If the latter, then the silhouette is all important, and adjustments will be needed to shape the body correctly together with bustles, hip rolls, crinolines, corsets, and stiffened petticoats.

In addition to style, period costumes require appropriate fabrics, colors, and trims if accuracy is to be achieved. Old fabrics may need to be sought out or newer fabrics given a distressed look by tea-dyeing or bleaching. Thus, designing an outfit becomes a series of choices. A combination of research into the background of the character being portrayed, an openness to ideas, and a willingness to experiment will all help with making decisions and ultimately contribute to the appeal of your doll.

There are no specific sewing techniques for constructing dolls' clothes, nor is any one method the "right way." Concentrate on eliminating unnecessary seams, reducing bulk wherever possible, and doing as much construction and decoration as possible while the garment is "flat," before side and sleeve seams are made. Whatever works and achieves the desired finished result is acceptable. The following guidelines will help you select the correct technique, while the projects highlight different aspects of dressmaking more fully.

SEAMS AND SEAM FINISHINGS

Flat seams and French seams are the most frequently made. Straight flat seams are pressed open, while curved seams are first clipped and then pressed to lie flat against the body. Edges are finished by zigzag, hand whipping, or in the case of delicate fabrics, by sealing with commercial edge sealer.

(**Right**) A French seam is a double seam with the raw edges enclosed between two lines of stitching. It is perfect for very narrow, straight, or gently curved seams on lightweight and sheer fabrics such as fine lawn for underwear. With wrong sides together, sew a narrow line within the seam allowance, trim and press to one side, then fold the garment to the wrong side on the sewing line. Finish the seam by sewing a second line on the seam allowance, thus enclosing the edges.

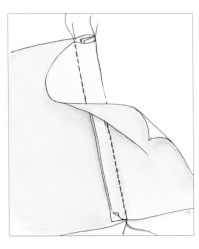

WORKING WITH THE BIAS

(**Above**) Cutting fabric on the bias or the cross, which is diagonal to the selvage, produces a piece of fabric with an edge that can be stretched. Usually this is avoided on large pieces, which can be difficult to work with if they are stretched out of place. However, narrow bias strips stretch easily to bind curved edges and slits, and can be used to make piping and frills that will stand out from a costume rather than lie flat against it. Using a striped fabric can produce some unusual effects. Sleeves for very small costumes constructed on the doll will be easier to handle if they are cut on the bias, since they will pull around the arm without any resistance.

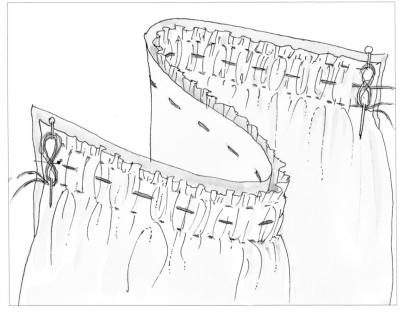

GATHERING

(**Above**) Gathers are used extensively for construction and decoration. Use a long stitch when making gathers for a seam and work two rows, one within the seam allowance and the other just outside it, leaving ends of thread at the start and finish. Mark the gathered edge in half and then quarters, then pull up the gathers within the seam allowance only. Adjust gathers to fit the edge to which they are being joined, then with the gathered edge uppermost, sew in place. Layer the seam and remove the lower row of gathering thread.

PRESSING AND IRONING

Costumes should be steam-pressed and ironed as they are constructed. In many cases it could be impossible to do this later. The size of the garments means that a regular ironing board will often be too big, and alternatives have to be found. Sleeveboards are ideal for larger costumes, while wooden rolling pins, dowels, and wooden spoon handles can all be padded and covered for smaller garments. Sandbags and pads of different sizes are also useful for fitting into awkward corners. Finally, for fabrics that should not be ironed, remember that finger pressing is an alternative, as is the flat end of a wooden modeling tool to press seams.

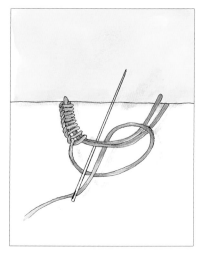

(**Above**) Buttonholes should be worked with fine thread. If the size is too small or the fabric is not suitable, work a buttonhole bar instead. Work a few foundation stitches on the surface of the fabric, each long enough to fit over the button. Then cover the threads with closely worked buttonhole stitches using the eye of the needle to work the stitch. A continuous line of these loops becomes an attractive edging.

LININGS AND FACINGS

Apart from costumes for larger dolls and straight-edge front or back openings which can have a folded facing, most costumes are too small for shaped facings. As an alternative, edges can be narrow-hemmed or rolled, bound with bias strips, or have a single fold covered with lace or gathered ribbon. If none of these is suitable, consider making a full lining from a sympathetic but thinner fabric. For example, stitch bodice and lining shoulder seams separately and then sew both together around neck and front or back openings. Then treat them as one fabric to complete the garment.

FASTENINGS

Tapes, ribbons, and buttons have all been used to fasten clothes for many hundreds of years. More recent inventions include hooks, snaps (press studs), safety pins, zippers, and elastic. Not all of these fasteners are suitable for small costumes, however, nor are some of them even produced in small sizes. You can make your own buttons from colored plastic using a hole punch or the smaller holes found in a leather punch.

TUCKS AND PLEATS

Tucks are folds of fabric stitched to hold their shape. Extremely fine tucks, known as pin tucks, are frequently used to decorate underwear. Deeper tucks can be a decorative feature as well as a way of shortening skirts that are too long.

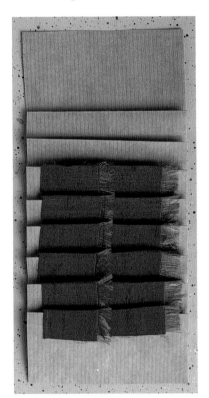

(**Left**) Pleats are folds that are pressed to hold their shape. Because they can be arranged in so many different and exciting ways, they are used extensively in making skirts and frills, and to decorate parts of garments. Make a brown paper template the required size of pleat. Then after decorating, lining, and/or hemming the fabric to be pleated, use the paper pleater as a pressing guide. Hide any seams inside a fold.

SMOCKING

(**Above**) Smocking is a pattern of embroidery stitches worked over a wide area of narrow pleats that have been made by working rows of evenly spaced gathers. Thus the gathers, which are being used to control fullness, also provide a basis for a decorative effect. Stitches are worked in stranded embroidery floss (cotton)—you will have to adjust the number of threads used according to the size of the costume being made. Very small dresses could have smocking worked with silk sewing thread to be in scale. Most general embroidery books give information about suitable stitches.

TRIMMING WITH RIBBONS

(**Left**) Ribbons provide an inexpensive way of adding color and interest to a costume. They can be used plain, folded, gathered, pleated, looped, woven, plaited, embroidered, or tied into bows and sashes.

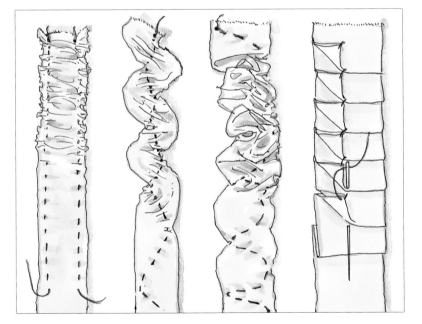

needle sculpture

SCULPTURED DOLLS, WHETHER MADE FROM HARD OR SOFT MATERIALS, ARE GENERALLY SHAPED WITHOUT PATTERNS. DECISIONS REGARDING AGE, SEX, SIZE, AND ANY SPECIAL FEATURES TO BE INCORPORATED INTO THE CHARACTER ARE MADE BEFORE YOU BEGIN, AND TOGETHER WITH AN UNDERSTANDING OF PROPORTIONS, THESE BECOME YOUR GUIDELINES AS YOU SHAPE, IN THIS CASE WITH NEEDLE AND THREAD.

Cossack, by English doll artist Lesley Roberts, has needle-sculptured face and hands.

Needle sculpture is both inspirational and full of surprises as each sculpture is unique, giving the dolls a special charm of their own. The technique is well suited to faces with strongly defined features such as the snub noses and rounded cheeks of babies and the wrinkles and folds of skin associated with aging.

Modelling with needle and thread is not dissimilar to working with clay, where you pinch, press, push and prod the modelling material, coaxing out the shape required. In this instance features are raised from a ball of stuffing, and tiny, almost invisible surface stitches hold the stuffing in place by a network of internal stitches that prevent the stuffing from springing back into the round shape. These stitches can be used both to indent and to raise ridges. The bridge of the nose is a good starting point for this kind of needle sculpture. Carry the thread from this point, invisibly through the head, ready to work the next feature. You must always be thinking ahead and planning the next move.

Another form of needle sculpture uses as a base a shaped ball of stuffing that could have an eyeline tied around it and extra pads of stuffing or halved foam balls added for cheeks. The stretchy skin fabric is then pulled over this foundation shape and shaping continues as before. Appliquéd features work well with needle sculpture, so a nose can be made separately from the head and then applied.

Yet another starting point is a shaped and stuffed head cut from a pattern where painted or embroidered features can be outlined or emphasized with the simplest of stitches. You can progress from shaped heads using fabrics with limited stretch to working with extremely stretchy fabrics containing a handful of unshaped stuffing. Try all the methods and combine them—needle sculpture needs practice to control shaping with tension.

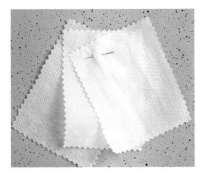

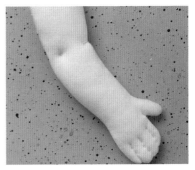

CONTROL OF STRETCH

(**Above**) Refer to page 13 to see how to measure the stretch of the fabric. Stretch can be controlled either by molding the stuffed head or limb, or by lining the fabric used for the body with iron-on nonwoven interfacing, which has some stretch as well; fine woven cotton fabric, which is firmer; and iron-on woven cotton, which gives maximum control, as the stretch is completely eliminated by the combination of firm fabric and glue.

THREADS

(**Above**) Use either hand-quilting thread, which is strong and not too thick, or polyester sewing thread. Use a single strand; doubled thread is more likely to tangle and form loops.

STITCHES

The two types of stitches used for needle sculpture are tiny $\frac{1}{16}$ in (1.5mm) stitches, which are then pulled tightly to shape the face or limb, and larger "loop" stitches, which carry the thread a longer way, form a specific feature such as the mouth or the crease of an elbow, and are generally pulled a bit less tight.

NEEDLE-SCULPTING ARMS

(**Above**) For the hand, needle-sculpt three lines to indicate four fingers by taking the needle up and down across the hand, pulling the stitches as you go. Make a small loop on the outside at the tip of the finger separations, and pull to indent clearly. Sculpt the wrist by running a "loop" stitch around the inner part of the wrist. For the elbows, run a short "loop" stitch on the inside of the arm at the elbow. Make two dimples by pushing the needle across from side to side, taking tiny stitches and pulling slightly, to indicate the hollows of the elbows.

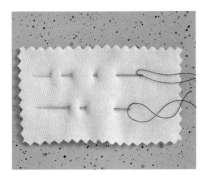

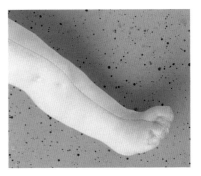

NEEDLES

(**Above**) Use thin, extra-long darning needles. Pliers help to pull the needle across the stuffing.

STRETCH FABRIC

(**Above**) Traditionally, nylon stockings were used, but now it is more common to use jersey fabric or stockinette. There are two types: double knit has no right and wrong side, while the right side of single knit shows as "knit" rows, and the wrong side as "purl" rows. Fabric that contains Lycra® stretches in both directions. (See also page 13.)

NEEDLE-SCULPTING LEGS

(**Above**) For the toes, mark the separations of the five toes with four loops going from the top to the bottom of the foot. For the ankle, insert the needle on one side and pull to the other, back and forth, to indent a small amount. Work knees as for elbows and make two dimples to indicate the sides of the knees.

TECHNIQUES FOR MAKING A NEEDLE-SCULPTED HEAD

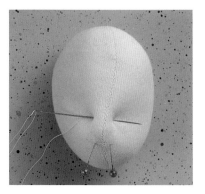

3. (**Above**) Insert the needle in the back of the head and bring it out at one entry point. Take a tiny stitch and come out at the entry point on the other side, pulling the thread at the same time. Repeat to secure in place.

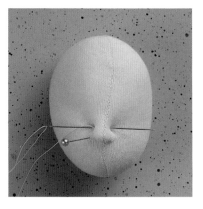

1. (**Above**) Make the head in stretch fabric, and stuff it as for any doll head. Mold it with your hands to give it a rounded shape. Move the stuffing into the nose by inserting a needle in the desired point and using a lever-type of movement. Use this technique as desired to put emphasis on different features, such as lips or cheeks. Find the area in the center of the head where the nose will be, and press with your fingers to "see" the shape where you are going to start sculpting.

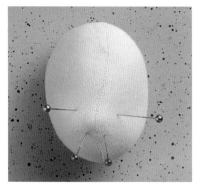

2. (**Above**) Establish the placement of the needle sculpture entry points—the corners where the bridge of the nose ends and the nostrils start—by marking them on both sides of the head with pins. Mark also the nostril openings. Do not remove the pins before inserting the needles once the thread is pulled on one side, it is very difficult to assess where the needle should go on the other side.

4. (**Above**) Make the nostrils by taking stitches from the nostril openings to the entry points. Shape the wider part of the nostrils with larger loop stitches on their outside edges. Bring more stuffing into them with the fine needle. The nose has a triangular shape, narrower at the top and wider at the nostrils. Take tiny stitches from side to side under the nose area, pulling the thread gently but tightly; the nose area will start to rise.

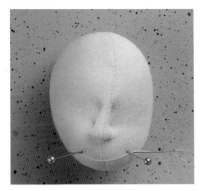

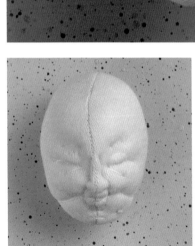

5. (**Above**) Use two pins to indicate the outer corners of the mouth, wider than the nose. Make a long stitch to indicate the parting of the lips; repeat.

6. (**Right**) If a prettier doll is wanted (like "Stretch Jersey Doll", page 103), paint the eyes and mouth now. Follow instructions for painting faces on pages 36–43.

7. (**Above**) Complete the needle sculpture by shaping the eyes and indenting the mouth. Insert the needle at the outer corners of the eyes and bring it out at the back of the head, forming an indentation where the head is going to be joined to the neck. Repeat to indent the inner corners of the eyes and the corners of the mouth. Do a few final stitches from the eye corners and the mouth corners.

8. (**Above**) If a more aged face is required, further stitches can be done: cheeks can be indented slightly; bags of skin can be produced with long loop stitches on the outside; eyelids and eyebrows can be emphasized with stitching. In this case it is better to leave the painting of the face until after the sculpting.

face masks

THE SOFTLY CONTOURED FEATURES PROVIDED BY FABRIC-COVERED FACE MASKS, WITHOUT A SEAM OR A STITCH IN SIGHT, ARE VERY APPEALING TO DOLLMAKERS WHO ARE NOT INSPIRED BY FLAT-FACED CLOTH DOLLS AND ARE OFTEN DAUNTED BY THE PROSPECT OF NEEDLE SCULPTURE.

Historically, several well-known dollmakers and manufacturers have used this technique to great advantage in the production of their dolls, such as the Italian Madame Lenci with her felt dolls, which were the epitome of the Art Deco period, Chad Valley and Norah Wellings of England, and Kathe Kruse, the German dollmaker who almost singlehandedly revolutionized the making of cloth dolls at the beginning of the twentieth century.

Felt, velveteen, and cotton, were the materials traditionally used for making masks, but nowadays knitted stretch fabrics are the most popular because they are so amenable. Modern white tacky glues are ideal for holding and stiffening cloth as it is being pressed over the features of a former, which can even be left in place if additional strength is needed. Commercially made fabric masks usually employ glue together with various heat and pressure processes.

There are many starting points, most of which are listed here (followed by detailed instructions for the preparation of some):
• Commercially made and painted plastic masks
• Fabric-covered, painted, and unpainted plastic masks
• Use an existing doll as a former to make your own mask.
• Make an original clay sculpture to use as a former
• Use a press mold to make a former (see pages 27 and 68).

With so many different ways to proceed, keep an open mind and experiment with methods and new materials. After all, trial and error has always been a good teacher.

USING PURCHASED HEAD MASKS
1. (**Right**) Ready-made masks come in different sizes. If they have a flat rim around them, trim it off first. A ready-painted fabric mask can be used as it is, by stitching it to the doll's one-piece head and body. Plastic masks are less attractive and are best re-covered with stretch fabric and painted.

Velveteen-bodied airman with cheerful face is typical of the dolls made by Norah Wellings.

2. Stretch jersey, preferably the stretchier stockinette or double jersey, is the best fabric to use as a top layer. It is advisable to use an intermediate layer of thin, open-mesh cotton (or two layers of stockinette) to stop the painted features from showing through the fabric. From each fabric, cut a rectangle a bit more than twice as wide as the mask and about 2 in (5cm) longer than the face. Round off the top corners and taper the sides toward the neck area.

3. (Right) Spread thick craft glue (PVA) evenly over the face and center the material on it. First glue the intermediate layer. Press down to make it stick, but do not pull sideways; make sure the fabric follows the shapes of the features and is well glued to the edges. Let it dry thoroughly. Then spread another coat of thick white glue, and place the stockinette layer onto it. Stroke gently to make it stick; never press hard, or the glue will seep through the fabric and the face will look blotchy. Let it dry well, and paint with acrylic or fabric paints.

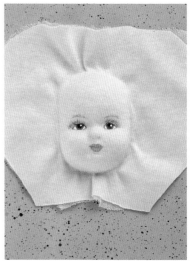

MAKING YOUR OWN MASKS

4. (Left) You will need a doll's head, either a plastic, ceramic, or porcelain one, or your own model, which could be made in modeling clay (Plasticine), pottery clay, or air-hardening clays. Choose a complete head, not one that lacks the top of the head like a traditional porcelain doll. If you use a child's plastic doll, it may be necessary to pluck some of the hair off, from the front to the top of the head. Dolls with moving eyes or eyelids are not suitable unless you remove them and block openings with clay. Ears may be included in the mask or not. It goes without saying that no valuable heads should be used for making masks— only use expendable ones.

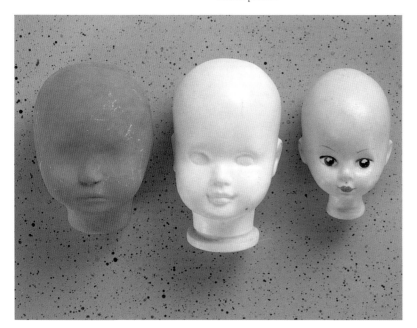

5. (Right) The mask is basically a combination of fabric and glue. The best material to use is buckram, a stiff hat-making material made of layers of open-mesh fabric and glue. The doll head, or at least its front section, should be smeared with a release agent, such as petroleum jelly, liquid detergent, or mold soap. Cut a piece of buckram about 1 in (25mm) larger all around than the doll's head and dip it in fairly hot water for about 10–15 seconds. Place it over the front of the head, well centered. Now work it into all the shapes of the features, and then smooth it over the neck and the sides. This procedure will take several minutes; at the beginning, it may feel that it will never stay in place, but it does. Help the process along by wetting your fingers from time to time, and use a smooth plastic stick to help flatten any creases. Leave to dry thoroughly overnight.

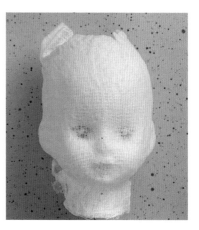

6. (**Right**) When dry, carefully remove the mask from the head and trim the rough edges. A layer of stockinette can now be glued to the mask, as explained in Step **3** on page 61; there is usually no need for an intermediate layer.

Sailor doll by Norah Wellings, with facial detail captured in a mask.

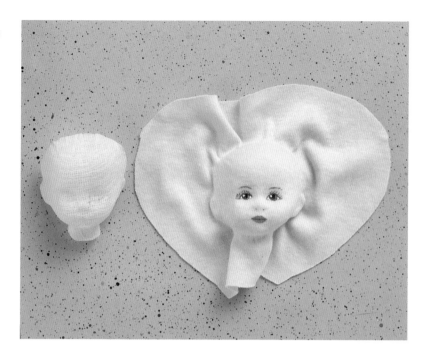

Felt doll by Alicia Merrett, with face mask, fur fabric hair and felt costume.

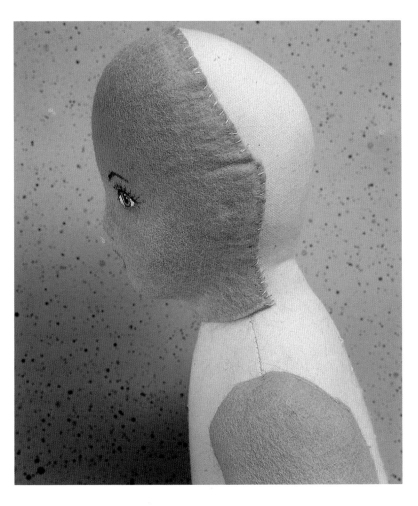

7. (Above) Masks can be also made by soaking thin cotton fabric cut on the bias in slightly diluted white glue (1 part water to 3 parts glue), and applying it to the head model, which has been smeared with a release agent as before. A second layer of fabric, or of torn paper soaked in glue (papier-mâché style), can be used to strengthen the mask further. Stockinette makes the best top layer.

8. (Left) The top layer can also be made from felt. Modern craft felt is thin and usually made from man-made fibers that are not as strong as the old-fashioned wool felt, so it is worth trying to obtain wool felt or one made with a mixture of wool and other fibers if possible. Cut a piece of felt about 1 in (25mm) bigger all around than the mask to be made. To make it more malleable, soak it in hot water for a few minutes. Squeeze it well, so the felt remains damp but not soaking wet. Cover the previously made buckram or fabric mask with a thick layer of white glue, and glue the felt to it. It will need more manipulation than a stockinette top layer, and it is usually necessary to hold the mask in place with rubber bands while it is drying. When it is half dry, remove the rubber bands. When it is fully dry—it may take 24 hours or more—trim the excess fabric and reinforce it by brushing a thick layer of glue inside the mask. Then paint the features.

ATTACHING THE MASK TO THE BODY

9. (Left) Although it is possible to make a back to the head, stuff it, and attach it to a body, it is far simpler to construct a body that includes an "inner" head all in one piece, to which the mask is then attached. First stuff the inner head and body very firmly, making sure the neck is really strong. If necessary, place a neck reinforcement inside it. Then attach the mask to the front, and stitch it in place with small stitches. It is fine to use flat inner heads when using purchased masks, which are relatively flat, but it is better to use more shaped inner heads when attaching masks made from rounder heads. A suitable body for this purpose is given in Felt Doll (page 106).

armatures

ARMATURES ARE SYSTEMS OF SUPPORT FOR BOTH STRENGTHENING AND POSING THE BODY. WHILE THEY ARE GENERALLY REGARDED AS THE "BONES" OF A DOLL THAT PROVIDE PERMANENT OVERALL SUPPORT AS SKELETONS OR UNATTACHED SUPPORT IN LOCALIZED AREAS, THERE ARE ALSO ARMATURES OF A MORE TEMPORARY NATURE. THESE WORKING ARMATURES PROVIDE SUPPORT DURING VARIOUS PROCESSES OF DOLLMAKING SUCH AS MODELING, FIRING, AND CURING.

Shepherd by the English doll artist Lorna Hennessey has an internal armature of aluminum wire.

Several factors will influence the need for armatures. It could be the size and weight of the doll, the materials or method used in the construction, the need to achieve a particular posture (such as a ballerina on point), or simply the need to enhance an essential gesture.

Larger dolls with cloth bodies and heavy heads such as those made from ceramic materials, wood, and air-drying clays, whether hollow or solid, will need more support than smaller cloth-bodied dolls. Narrow areas are always potential weak points, especially. When stuffing alone does not support the head, you may need to cut a wider neck. While this may solve the problem physically, it could be wrong esthetically. A new strategy may be needed, such as providing an unattached armature such as a dowel rod inserted with the stuffing.

A similar problem exists when a doll with cloth legs is displayed standing. The conventional stand is unsightly and gets in the way of the display and detracts unnecessarily. An internal armature would overcome the problem, or rods, that pass through the feet and into the legs, can be set in a board base. Dolls with long dresses do not need legs. Stuffed and weighted petticoats or rods reaching from base to waist can provide support.

Body armature is such an integral part of the doll that it must be thoroughly considered at the designing stage. Decisions need to be made about how the armature is to be anchored, whether limbs should be hollow for wires and grooves made for tying on cloth skins, or whether the doll is to be formed by wrapping batting (wadding) around a skeleton. Because working armatures are temporary, they can always be improvised as work progresses. Anything that works can be used.

MATERIALS FOR ARMATURES

(**Right**) While the vast majority of armatures are custom-made by the doll artist, there are a number available through ceramic doll studios. An increasingly popular skeleton is a system composed of interlocking plastic beads. These beads are shaped so that they lock together but remain flexible throughout their length, allowing a doll to be posed as required and the position maintained or recovered at will. The disadvantages are restricted size range and cost; they are somewhat expensive. In addition, there are various combinations of metal plate and plate with wire skeletons available commercially. These are all bendable to a certain extent, but some are better regarded as formers. Once they are bent into shape, the doll retains that posture. Plates for hands allow dolls to grasp and hold objects. Again, sizes and selection are limited.

Consequently, most doll artists construct their own armatures with the needs of the specific doll in mind. The most frequently used materials are those found around the house or in local hardware stores and include wire of all kinds and thicknesses, wood as doweling rods, paper and cardboard, plastic sheets, Styrofoam (polystyrene) balls and cotton balls, foil, pipe cleaners, rolled cloth, plastic tubing, and artists' flexible curves.

Wire comes in many different gauges, is easy to cut and shape, and requires few tools other than pliers and wire cutters. The wire you choose should take into account whether it will be constantly flexed or not. For dolls between 6 in (15cm) and 12 in (30cm) tall, a 16-gauge galvanized wire is a good choice. Smaller dolls take a finer (even copper) wire, while for larger dolls, you can double the wire. Remember, the higher the gauge number, the thinner the wire. Perhaps the best wire, even though it is more expensive, is a lightweight but very strong and flexible aluminum alloy used by artists. Sold in three gauges, it can be found in art-supply stores.

WORKING ARMATURES FOR HEADS

(**Left**) A simple armature for modeling heads is a hand-held length of dowel with a core, shaped roughly like a head on one end. This reduces the amount and therefore thickness of clay needed. Removing the dowel means the core material can be removed so the head dries quicker and of course is lighter in weight. Suitable materials for cores are wound and bound paper, crumpled aluminum foil, Styrofoam (polystyrene) balls and cotton balls, and even corrugated cardboard. A former of modeling clay (Plasticine), although not so quickly made, is also worth considering.

BODY ARMATURES

There are examples of body armature illustrated throughout the book, and detailed instructions for making two of them are given with projects. Santa Claus (page 119) has both armature and body skin fixed to the limbs and stuffing inserted inside the skin to surround the armature. Hannah (page 116) has no body skin; her form consists of batting wrapped around the wires until the desired shape is achieved.

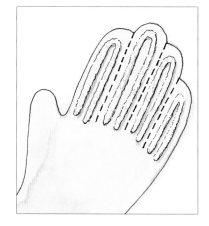

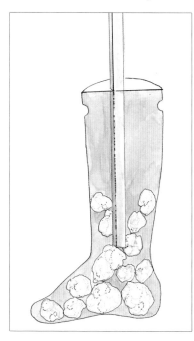

(**Left**) To set wires, the limbs are half filled with Styrofoam (polystyrene) chips, then the wires are embedded. The position is made rigid by filling the top half of the limbs with either quick-setting compound or epoxy putty; make sure the latter is pushed firmly against the inside wall of the limbs and that the wires are central.

(**Above**) Make arms as directed by pattern instructions, topstitching finger channels. Cut four lengths of pipe cleaner, each twice the length of its finger, then bend in half and insert in respective channels. Take up any slackness in the channel either by inserting wisps of stuffing or by removing pipe cleaners and wrapping them with yarn, then reinserting.

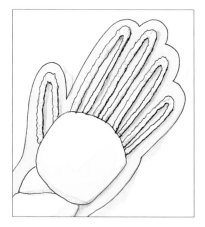

Whatever form of armature you choose, always try to construct it with a full-size plan of the body drawn out so that wires can be laid down for reference. Shoulder width is one and a half times the length of the head, and wires should bend at right angles to form the arms. Legs drop from the hips and lie just within the shoulder width. Armatures that have width at the shoulders and hips will have limbs that hang more realistically, and clothes will also hang better.

HAND ARMATURES

After faces, hands are probably the next most expressive part of the body. Their every gesture contributes to the appeal of a doll. Thus, being able to bend fingers is an attractive option for dollmakers.

For cloth dolls with a simple mitten hand—that is, the four fingers closed together and a separate thumb—the solution can be achieved with pipe cleaners, provided each finger is at least as wide as a doubled pipe cleaner. Very wide fingers on larger dolls may need doubled pipe cleaners.

(**Above**) A wrist greatly increases the amount of movement possible. For each finger cut a pipe cleaner long enough when doubled to reach from palm to fingertip and then single to the middle of the forearm. Bind the fingers together by gluing felt pads on each side of the palm. Then wrap the lower arm section in a narrow strip of batting and insert it in a cloth arm. Continue as directed.

A hand board is a simple wooden construction which can be used over and over to make pairs of hands where fingers are separate and both hands the same size. It's a good idea to make several in different sizes for small and large dolls. You will need a flat piece of wood, several nails, a hammer, and a pattern of the hand.

(**Right**) Trace the hand outline on the board, then hammer in nails at the top and bottom of the fingers and down the sides of the hand. Leave the heads of the nails above the wood. Using a flexible wire (thin for small hands and thicker for large ones), bend the wire to follow the nails and cut it off beyond the wrist. Carefully remove the wire from the frame.

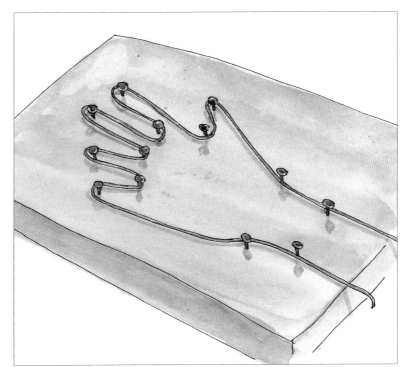

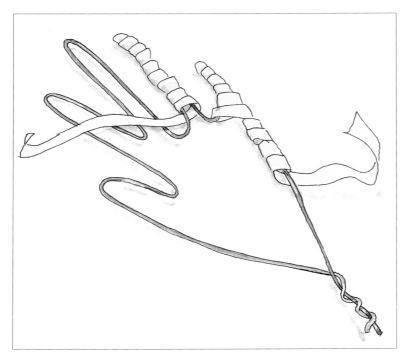

(**Left**) Twist the cut ends of the wire several times, then wrap strips of bandage or batting around the frame. If the hand is to be used for a cloth doll, then simply continue covering the armature, building up the shape, covering the palm, and inserting it into the stitched arm before bending the fingers. The same armature can also be used for modeling by first bending the fingers and hand into the desired position and then covering with a thin layer of glue before applying air-drying clay or plastic wood.

molds and press molds

MOLDS ARE USED TO MAKE MULTIPLE REPRODUCTIONS OF SCULPTURED DOLLS, EITHER THE HEAD AND LOWER LIMBS OR A COMPLETE BODY. THEY ARE, IN EFFECT, THE "PATTERN," WHEREBY LIQUIDS SUCH AS PORCELAIN SLIP, COMPOSITION, AND MELTED WAX CAN BE CAST IN A PLASTER MOLD TO PRODUCE A SKIN THAT REPLICATES ALL THE DETAILS OF THE MOLD.

It is also possible to make face masks by pressing various modeling materials into the face area of such a mold, which again replicates the contours and holds the shape after air-drying or curing.

Making and using molds need be neither daunting nor expensive. While plaster is still the most popular material for mold-making, there are newer products available that are less messy to work with than plaster. This also means that many other liquid materials can be considered in addition to the traditional ceramic slips used for bisque dolls and melted wax, both of which were used to make exquisite dolls in the nineteenth century and which are still being used by modern doll artists. Some of the newer casting materials are improved compositions, resins, papier-mâché casting slip, and latex.

Many dollmaking studios stock a vast choice of plaster molds for both reproduction and modern dolls, as well as casting slips and the plaster for making molds. It is possible to buy reasonably priced molds for heads that can be used with materials other than porcelain slip, which is outside the scope of this book. Also consider looking for other sources of suitable materials, such as cake decorating suppliers selling plastic molds that can be used with "cold porcelain" to make cabinet and dolls' house dolls, and suppliers of sculpture materials stocking modeling and casting materials. Stuffed toymaking suppliers stock plastic faces for covering with fabric, some of which can be used successfully either to make face molds or as press molds.

Gretchen by Kammer and Reinhardt, a small all-bisque doll with every part of the body cast in a mold. Doll reproduced by the author and costumed by Nyola Warnes.

(Right) Using a hard-headed doll, such as one made of plastic, as a starting point is an easy way to explore the potential of making your own molds. The chosen head should have fixed eyes, a closed mouth, and no eyelashes, while wigs should be pulled off or hair shaved away from the forehead at least back to the part line. This line divides the front from the back of the head and is where the mold would have separated into two parts to make the original hard head. It will always start at the neck on one side and pass up and over the head at the widest point, which is generally between the ears. Mark this line on your model with a pencil or pen.

It is absolutely vital that this line is correctly identified when making a mold of two or more parts, because any obstruction caused by the model will prevent the mold from being withdrawn. The position of the part line is less critical when making the one-part molds described here.

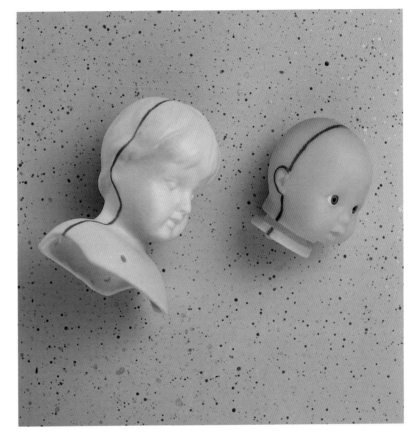

MAKING A QUICK-IMPRESSION MOLD

1. This quick method is ideal for making molds for small dolls. Take a block of colored polymer clay such as Fimo or Sculpey about the size of a lemon, and work it in your hands until it is pliable. Now pat it flat and roll it on a piece of waxed paper, making a thick slab about 1¼ in (32mm) deep. Turn it over so the flat, smooth side with no cracks is uppermost.

2. Prepare your plastic head, then dust the face with talcum powder (see above left) so it will not stick to the clay. Press the powdered face straight down into the clay until it reaches the part line. Pull it back out, straight up. Inspect the mold, and if you are happy with the image, cure the clay according to the manufacturer's instructions. Cool before using.

3. Dust the inside of the mold with powder. Work a walnut-sized piece of flesh-colored polymer clay smooth, then push it firmly into the mold and pull straight out. If the impression is not good enough, try again. Powder the mold each time. Small flaws can be smoothed over, but unsightly flaws that keep appearing are a fault in the mold (which will have to be remade).

MAKING A ONE-PART PLASTER MOLD

2. (Below) Secure the face or head, face up, in a stable horizontal position on a flat working surface that is covered with a thick plastic sheet. Put some water into a plastic bowl or bucket, sprinkle plaster of Paris into the water until it forms a pyramid with the tip projecting above the surface, then mix. When the plaster starts to thicken, dribble a thin layer onto the head, taking care to avoid any air bubbles. Continue adding plaster until the head is covered to a depth of approximately 1½ in (4cm) as shown. Try to keep the top relatively flat. Let the mold dry for a few hours before removing it from the head, then set it aside to finish drying.

1. (Above) If you are using an existing hard head, the face will have to be isolated from the back. Embed the back in a deep bed of modeling clay that reaches up to the part line, leaving just the face exposed. The clay should also extend out beyond the head by 2 in (5cm). More exciting is to use your original clay sculptured head, prepared by placing a collar of thin, wedge-shaped brass separators, overlapping as shown, around the part line. Both heads should be smeared with a thin covering of mold soap or petroleum jelly, which acts as the release agent.

Leave any plaster remaining in the bowl to harden, then flex the sides of the bowl to release and dispose of the slab. Excess plaster should never be poured down a sink or toilet as it will set in the discharge pipes. To use this mold as a press mold for face masks, you must first smear the surface of the plaster with a thin layer of petroleum jelly to prevent the mask material from sticking to the plaster. Modeling materials like air-drying clays and plastic wood can be used either as slabs which drape in the mold or by pushing in chunk by chunk and building up a covering layer. The technique employed will depend on the nature of the material being used.

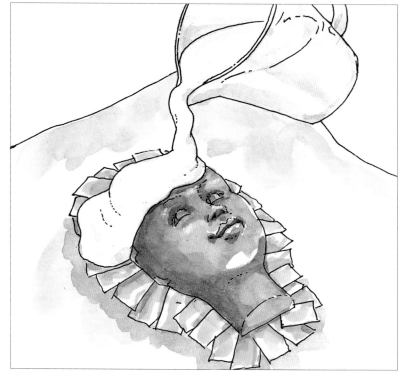

3. (Left) All these materials can be left in place to dry and then removed, cleaned, sanded, and painted, or covered with a fabric skin which in turn is painted. It is possible to make face masks in these molds with polymer clays—be careful when removing them so the features are not scuffed. These clays need to be cured in the oven. (See page 25 for more information.)

Shown here is a Fimo pancake being pushed into the detailed crevices of the face.

4. (Below) Liquid casting materials such as latex, composition, melted wax, and papier-mâché casting slip can all be used in this plaster mold. In this instance, the plaster should be thoroughly clean and free from petroleum jelly, never having been used as a press mold. All liquids (except wax) are poured into a dry mold and left for differing times until a "skin" is formed. Follow manufacturers' recommendations for timing and thickness of cast. Some topping off may be needed, then excess liquids should be returned to containers for recycling. Leave castings to harden before removing from the mold.

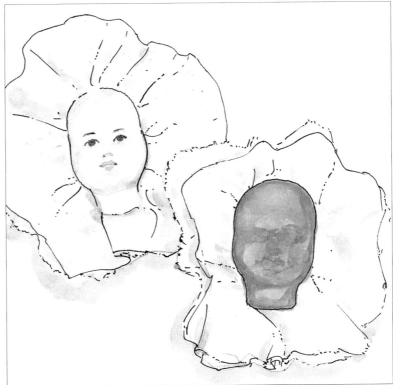

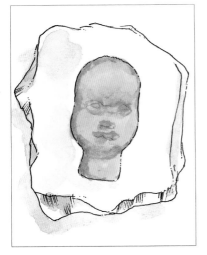

5. (Above) Trim edges and cover latex and composition masks with fabric according to dollmaking instructions. Papier-mâché masks can be used as they are, or sanded, sealed, and painted. Wax is heated and poured into a damp mold and finished again, according to manufacturers' recommendations.

Aaron by Diana Effner, reproduced by the author and costumed by Susan Baker.

paper and papier-mâché

THE GREAT ATTRACTION OF PAPER FOR CHILDREN AND ADULTS ALIKE IS ITS CHEAPNESS AND VERSATILITY. SIMPLE TECHNIQUES OF CUTTING, FOLDING, PADDING, STITCHING, AND GLUING CAN ALL BE USED TO MAKE DOLLS, WHILE PROCESSED PAPER PULP OFFERS ADDITIONAL CHALLENGES IN THE FORM OF A CLAYLIKE MODELING MATERIAL AND A CASTING SLIP THAT CAN BE USED WITH MOLDS.

The earliest known surviving European paper dolls are the animated French Pantins, supposedly from about 1746. Known in England as Jumping Jacks and in Germany as Hamplemann, they are all paper or wooden dolls loosely jointed together which can be made to dance by pulling a string that jerks the limbs. These very collectible dolls, originally sold as printed sheets either uncolored or handcolored, became such a fashionable craze at the French court that the police eventually banned them for fear of the effect they would have on pregnant women. Despite such drastic measures, Jumping Jacks are still made today, usually as nursery toys, while American doll artists are presently reinventing them as fabric-dressed paper dolls called Paper Nellas.

Other popular flat paper and cardboard dolls from this time were French soldiers for war games, fashion mannequins for adults, and paper dolls with complete wardrobes for children. Toward the end of the nineteenth century, a more economical method of printing color was developed and this made these dolls more affordable. Their popularity is still evident today with the mass production of paper dolls depicting film stars, famous people, and historical characters.

A selection of four of the legendary Immortals. Notice the delicately painted features.

(**Right**) Since paper and papier-mâché are both products of the Far East, it is not surprising that many of these countries have a strong tradition involving paper dolls both for play and ritual purposes. From China come the Immortals, a set of eight legendary male characters that have been made as dolls for hundreds of years. Each character is a paper-based doll dressed in a lightly padded silk costume; the faces were originally painted on silk, but now are more likely to be drawn on paper. The characters hold paper objects that serve to identify them, while the hair and beards are made from real hair.

Origami, the art of folding paper, was introduced to Japan from China in the sixteenth century, and the wonderful array of traditional Japanese papers has inspired craftsmen to use it extensively in dollmaking. There are ceremonial paper dolls as well as dolls for play. Anesama dolls, originally developed as educational aids for teaching the courtesies of dining and entertaining guests, have plain and patterned paper costumes with padded heads and elaborate hairstyles. Simpler paper dolls, Kami Ningyo, are generally made from flat folded paper with featureless faces and are often exhibited from the back.

Modern origami papers, attractively displayed with all designs clearly visible.

PAPIER-MÂCHÉ

Many kinds of paper-based products, and several different techniques, are referred to, somewhat confusingly, as "papier-mâché." These include pressed paper constructions, modeling with pulp and paper strips, either using paper alone or combining it with fillers to add strength and cut the cost, or with glues to bind it all together. Essentially, papier-mâché is a much stronger and more durable product than conventional flat paper and will hold its shape when it dries. With these properties it is not surprising that papier-mâché became a cheap alternative for wood and was used to make inexpensive furniture, boxes, household items, and dolls.

Simple Japanese paper dolls.

PAPIER-MÂCHÉ PULP During the 1800s papier-mâché pulp was probably the most widely used form of composition for making dolls, as it was malleable and could be pressed into molds to make hollow limbs and heads. Although there are many different methods and recipes used to prepare pulp, the instructions on page 83 (Modeling) will produce a pulp that can be used in the following ways:
• To model an original doll.
• Pressed into molds to make duplicate dolls.
• Pressed into a face mold to make a mask.
• Pressed around a doll to make a mold.
• Pressed against a face to make a mold for duplicating masks.

LAMINATED PAPIER-MÂCHÉ Gluing layers of paper together over a former to make heads is a popular method among doll artists and puppet makers. The technique favors strongly defined features like jaws and noses, as the effect of successive layers of paper lessens fine detail. Some doll artists achieve high levels of workmanship with this technique, although others regard it as messy and best reserved for the classroom.

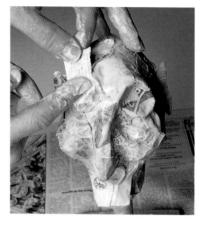

1. Laminated paper is worked over a former, which can be an existing doll or a clay sculpture supported on an armature. Keep the features strong and simple and make a neck that splays out to form a flange. Cover the clay with 1-in (25mm) squares of dampened tissue paper or with petroleum jelly, both of which prevent papier-mâché from sticking to the clay.

2. Cover the head with at least six layers of postage stamp-size squares of torn newspaper glued together with craft glue (PVA) or wallpaper paste. Complete each layer before starting a new one, adding a layer of colored tissue to check on how evenly you are working. Smooth the paper with the fingers to remove wrinkles and air bubbles and to blend all edges together.

3. When the head is thoroughly dry, cut it in half from side to side, behind the ears and over the crown. A small V-shaped cut on the top of the head will assist in realigning the halves together. Scoop out the clay and set it aside for future projects. Any weak areas in the head can be strengthened with more paper and paste, plastic wood, or glue.

4. (**Right**) Rejoin the head and strengthen the neck edge by covering it with layers of paper and paste or glue. When the head is dry, it can be cut and drilled to make eye sockets and for mounting earrings, and the surface can be smoothed by sanding. A layer of gesso will also smooth the surface and act as a primer for painting. Otherwise, paint with latex (emulsion) prior to painting skin tone and features.

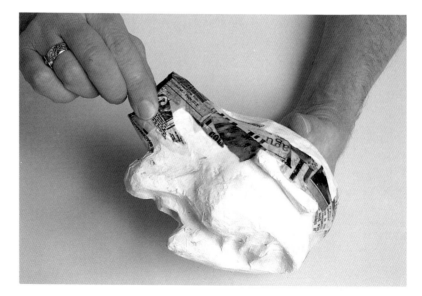

PAPIER-MÂCHÉ CASTING SLIP Paper pulp processed to the consistency of a fine liquid can be used in almost the same way as porcelain casting slips using the same molds. It is a relatively hard material, scratch resistant, lightweight, reasonably heat and damp resistant, pleasant to touch, and easy to paint. The same slip can also be thickened and used as a modeling material to build up layers of hair or alter facial features. More importantly, it does not need to be kiln-fired, so dollmakers are able to produce dolls from molds inexpensively.

The slip must be prepared by thorough stirring and then thinned with water until it has the consistency of thin pancake batter. Pour it into a pitcher and let it settle so all air bubbles rise to the surface. Prepare molds by lightly spraying with water, then fill them with slip and leave for 2 to 3 minutes, but all the while keeping the level by topping off with more slip.

holes, and any unwanted extras using a scalpel and wet paint brush. Final cleaning involves smoothing the surface with fine sandpaper or a scrub sponge (grit scrubber) when the parts are dry.

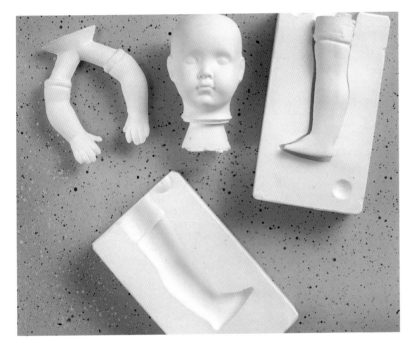

3. (Above) Seal the surface or paint a basic skin tone directly onto the doll before finishing with features and setting in eyes. Papier-mâché casting slip is enhanced by waxing lightly and buffing to give a healthy sheen.

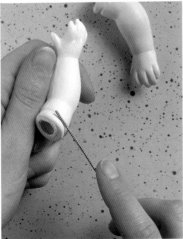

1. (Above) Empty out the slip and leave the mold to drain for 1 to 2 hours. By this time the slip will have come away from the wall of the mold, which can be opened and the supported cast left in mold half to dry further. When the cast is firm enough to handle, it can be removed, and as much cleaning as possible should be done at this time.

2. (Right) Fill in holes by applying slip with a paint brush, cut out eye and mouth openings with a scalpel, and seal edges with a wet paint brush. Then clean off seams, flanges from the pour

Andrea by Helga Matejka, a Glorex papier-mâché Kit. Doll painted and costumed by Lorna Whitaker.

working with wood

WOOD, BEING A NATURAL MATERIAL AND READILY AVAILABLE, HAS BEEN USED BY CRAFTSMEN ALL OVER THE WORLD FOR COUNTLESS CENTURIES, SUPPORTING A STRONG TRADITION OF FOLK DOLLS, VOTIVE IMAGES, AND TALISMANS AS WELL AS DOLLS FOR PLEASURE. AS AN INDUSTRY, DOLLMAKING WAS WELL UNDERWAY BY THE SEVENTEENTH CENTURY. DOLLS MADE AT THIS TIME WERE THE EXCLUSIVE ENGLISH QUEEN ANNE DOLLS WITH INSET GLASS EYES AND FASHIONABLE COSTUMES AND THE MORE CHEAPLY PRODUCED EUROPEAN PEG WOODENS MADE BY FORESTERS DURING THE WINTER MONTHS AND THEN SOLD BY PEDDLERS.

Wooden dolls can be fashioned quickly and easily from found wood and decorated with other naturally occurring materials like moss, twine, nuts, shells, feathers, and fur, or with scraps of fabric where there is a weaving tradition. More often, however, wood will be carefully selected and then either handcarved or turned on a lathe. Dolls made on lathes are generally the work of craftsmen, long skilled in their art, whether for making folk dolls like the Russian nesting Matroyshkas, individually crafted artist dolls, or the mass-produced and inexpensive skittle people, which are not much more than dolls without arms or legs. These basic bodies are often turned over to other workers who take on the painting and completion.

Carving, however, is more accessible to would-be dollmakers, especially whittling, which is shaping a piece of handheld wood with a knife. Traditional carving employs various gouges and chisels, with the doll often supported in a vise throughout the work. Choosing a suitable wood will depend on the tools being used and how the doll is going to be constructed. Obviously, it should be malleable enough to work with and accept fine detail, yet it must also be strong and durable and able to take a good finish.

Hopi Kachinas made from drift cottonwood root by Narron Lomayaktewa.

(**Above and left**) A different approach altogether is to use a ready-made wooden article or finial as the basis for a doll, a solution that has been adopted time and time again. Thread spools (cotton reels), wooden spoons, and old-fashioned clothespins (pegs) have long been used in this way, and by following this course of action you will be able to experience simple carving and painting techniques used for working with wood.

SPOON HEADS

Wooden spoons have a perfect face area waiting to be decorated and are a good way to experiment with painting with acrylics, mixing flesh colors, drawing faces, and then putting it all together. You can use successful heads to make the dolls on page 111 (Spoon Doll), while unsatisfactory heads can be sanded down and started over again.

1. (**Left**) Prepare the back of the spoon by sanding gently so that it is very smooth, then wipe away any wood dust. Seal the surface of the wood with acrylic gesso or primer and when that is dry, sand again to give a perfectly smooth surface for painting. Mix a flesh color (page 43) and apply. Allow an hour for it to dry and then apply a second coat to get a good coverage.

2. (**Right**) Practice drawing on paper faces that would fit the spoon. When you are happy with the results, transfer the best face to the spoon. Start by painting the whites of the eyes and slowly build up all the other features, letting each color dry in turn before adding more detail. Finish by painting on an outline of hair to frame the face, and when the paint is thoroughly dry, seal it with several coats of clear acrylic spray.

CLOTHESPIN (PEG) DOLLS

Old-fashioned clothespins (pegs) are a natural for dollmaking. With head, torso, and legs already in place, they are just waiting to be converted into dolls by adding arms and a face. To make this a clown, you will need in addition to the clothespin (peg) the following tools: a coping saw, sandpaper (grit no. 2), sandplate (optional), cloth, hand drill, and craft knife. Extra height on the top of the head is modeled with plastic wood, which is smoothed with acetone (nail polish remover), then the whole clothespin is decorated with acrylic paints and ribbon.

You will need the following materials to make the clothespin (peg) doll:
• Clothespin (peg)
• Pencil
• Coping saw
• Sandpaper
• Cloth
• Hand drill
• Craft knife
• Needle
• Plastic wood
• Acetone
• Acrylic gesso or primer
• Paint brushes
• Acrylic paints
• Felt for hair
• Ribbon for neck ruff
• Copper wire or thin elastic
• Jeweler's pliers
• Spacer key
• Glue

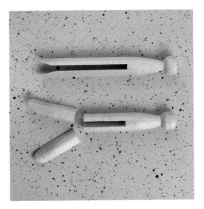

1. (Left) Before cutting the clothespin, have a good look at it and decide which is to be the front. Mark this side with a small pencil cross. Now shorten the peg to 3 in (7.5cm) by sawing off the bottom of the legs. Select the best cut-off to become the arms and discard the other.

2. (Above) The arm piece may need shortening. Hold the arm piece to the body and, remembering that wrists will be level with tops of legs, measure how much to cut off. The example shown was shortened by ¼ in (6mm). Lay the arm flat and saw in half lengthwise to make two arms. Note that you have a pair.

3. (Right) Holding the head of the clothespin securely in one hand, use a craft knife to whittle away the front edges of the legs from the waist down to the feet. This will follow the direction of the grain. Always whittle away from your own body to avoid accidents. Make sure that the clothespin will stand, and if it doesn't, sand the bottom until both feet are level.

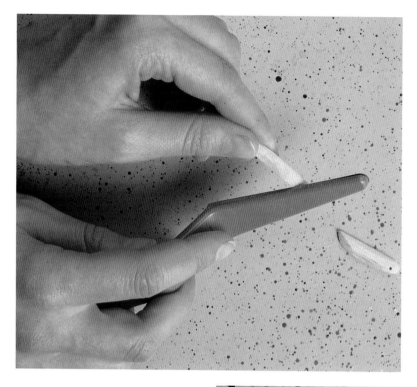

4. (Left) The arms are triangular in cross section with the ridge on the underside, lying next to the body. Remove this ridge by sanding with a sandplate for speed or more slowly with sandpaper. Keep sanding until the inside of the arm is flat. Round off the shoulders by first whittling to remove excess wood, then sand to make a really smooth surface. Drill a hole through the top of each arm.

5. (Right) Place the arms against the body and mark the position of the holes with a needle. Then drill matching holes right through the body. Sand the surface and clean out all the holes thoroughly. Use plastic wood to build up shape of head and make a small ball for the nose, positioning it on the front side of the clothespin. Smooth with acetone at this point rather than using sandpaper later. Leave to set overnight.

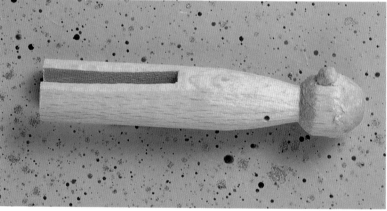

6. Sand the modeled area as necessary. Remove wood dust with a cloth, then prime the wood with acrylic gesso or another water-based primer. Painting is a matter of personal choice—you will choose your own colors to suit the character. Keep colors pure and intense for clowns, applying several layers rather than one thick coat. Acrylics dry very quickly and the next coat can be put on after 20 minutes.

7. (Right) Lightly draw in the outline of eyes and mouth and any pattern that is needed for slacks and shirt, then paint using fine brushes for more detailed work. Thread wet freshly painted pieces onto a thin wire and suspend between supports to dry without touching.

8. The arms and body can be joined together in several ways but the following are probably the most satisfactory.

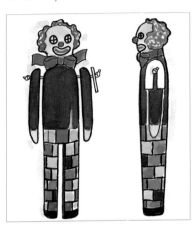

8a. (Above) Using jeweler's pliers, turn a small loop on the end of a piece of copper wire. Pass the unturned end through all three elements of the doll plus a cardboard spacer key and lock the end of the wire by cutting and forming another loop. Press both loops flat against the arms; remove spacer key.

8b. (Above) Tie a knot in the end of a length of thin elastic, then feed the other end through all three elements. Make another knot. Before pulling it tight, place a needle through the loop and slide the knot up tight against the arm. Pull tight to fasten off, removing the needle. Trim elastic and seal knots.

Simple checkerboard colored transfers for the clown have been offset with a plain top and red ribbon for the neck bow. The same ribbon has been unraveled to make matching curls.

9. Your clown is now ready for the finishing touches—a piece of felt or thread curls for hair, a ribbon ruff or bow at the neck, and perhaps a painted cardboard hat. With a little imagination, these simple clothespins can be transformed in so many ways that it is no wonder that they remain popular for dollmakers and firm favorites with children.

modeling

BEING ABLE TO MODEL YOUR OWN DOLLS IS ONE OF THE MOST
SATISFYING ASPECTS OF DOLLMAKING, FOR YOU ARE THEN
COMPLETELY FREE TO MAKE YOUR OWN DECISIONS REGARDING
EVERY ASPECT OF THE DOLL, PRODUCING AN ENTIRELY ORIGINAL
PIECE OF WORK. DOLLS MADE FROM PATTERNS AND MOLDS MAY FREE
YOU FROM HAVING TO MAKE MAJOR DESIGN DECISIONS, BUT
WHAT YOU MAKE WILL BE A COPY.

Modeling is not difficult, especially since there are
so many different kinds of modeling materials to
choose from. They should all fulfill certain basic
requirements. You should be able to knead
them easily between your fingers, and, after
shaping, the material should dry or cure hard
and be stable and durable. You should then
be able to work on it further, refining the
surface by sanding and smoothing and then
finish by painting and sealing.

MODELING MATERIALS

There are several modeling mixtures
that you can make for yourself and
experiment with to gain confidence.
The recipes given here use sawdust,
bread, and paper respectively. Each basic
ingredient is then combined with other
substances to make an acceptable modeling
material.

Sawdust paste or pâte de bois

1. Sift the finest sawdust possible into a
bowl. In a second bowl, prepare a small
quantity of thick wallpaper paste according
to manufacturer's instructions. Add paste to
the sawdust and mix together until you can
remove it from the bowl like a slab of pastry.
Continue kneading it well, adding more
sawdust if it feels too sticky on your fingers.
This paste must be used immediately and
cannot be stored for future use.

Prospero by Julia Hills is a clay-headed doll dressed in a
costume that reflects Julia's training in theatre design.

2. Thoroughly wet the finest sawdust available and squeeze out excess water. Add white wood glue and mix together until you have a manageable modeling consistency.

Bread dough

Flour dough is one of the oldest modeling materials, and this recipe is a modern version that is particularly suitable for small dolls.

- 3 slices of bread with crusts removed
- 2 tablespoons of white craft glue
- 1 teaspoon of glycerin
- few drops of preservative such as formaldehyde, sodium citrate, or oil of wintergreen

Shred bread to fine crumbs and mix thoroughly with other ingredients. Wrapped in plastic film, this dough will keep in the refrigerator and freezes successfully.

Papier-mâché paste

Tear a newspaper into postage stamp-size squares, place in a bucket, cover with warm water, stir vigorously to separate pieces of paper, and then leave to soak overnight. Wearing rubber gloves, remove handfuls of pulp and squeeze firmly to remove water. Place in a strainer and drain further. This is the basic pulp.

Put 2 cups of pulp in a kitchen blender with 2 tablespoons of white craft glue. Blend thoroughly, adding a little soaking water to help the blades rotate. Do not be tempted to pour the soaking water sludge down a drain. Wrap it and put it in a trash can.

Clays

The new low-temperature polymer clays are a real boon to the doll artist. Clean and dry to work with, they have positively revolutionized dollmaking. They come ready to use in flesh colors, and dolls can be modeled, cured, and painted within a day. However, they pick up dirt easily, so make sure that your hands and work area are both kept scrupulously clean.

Air-drying clays are, like natural clays, somewhat damp to work with, but they are more even in texture and carefully formulated for strength. Work should be kept covered with a damp cloth in a sealed plastic bag when left unattended to prevent drying. These clays take several days to dry out thoroughly and need to have a flesh color added before features can be put on.

Plastic wood

Plastic wood is coarser than clay, but it is particularly strong. Use it over a core head of modeling clay (Plasticine) that has been smeared with petroleum jelly to act as a release agent. Rubbing the surface with nail polish remover makes it easier to model, and the finished surface will be smoother. Heads modeled with plastic wood can be sawn in half when they are dry, so the former can be removed. The halves are then glued back together.

Making layers

Virtually all these modeling materials should be used in layers approximately $\frac{1}{4}$ in (6mm) thick. More of the substance can nearly always be added to build up areas or fill in cracks, but the surface may need to be scored to form a key, or dampened, or even glued before you continue. Follow manufacturer's recommendations and don't be afraid to experiment.

Modeling a doll can only begin after a series of decisions have been reached. You must decide the sex, age, overall size, parts to be modeled, parts to be made from cloth, whether it will have an armature or not, how the sculptured parts are to be attached to the body, and so on.

Proportions need to be considered and a decision made about which modeling material to use. Armed with all this information, plus pictures, photographs, and other source material you have researched, you still have to decide whether your modeling is to be true to life and realistic, abstract and fanciful, or simple and basic.

Before you dismiss sculpture as being too difficult, you should at least try it. Explore the possibilities of modeling very basic heads from the wide variety of materials available until you find the medium that works best for you. By carefully following the steps outlined here, you will have a perfectly acceptable doll. Practice and experience will make you adventurous, and as your confidence grows, the dolls will move from basic to realistic.

Strong features in clay by doll artist Ella Maija Laitasalo.

modeling basic heads and limbs

THINK OF THE HEAD AS BEING MADE IN FOUR STAGES: FIRST IS THE CORE OR ARMATURE, FOLLOWED BY A BASIC HEAD AND NECK SHAPE, THEN FEATURES, AND FINALLY THE FLANGE OR SHOULDER PLATE BY WHICH THE HEAD WILL BE ATTACHED TO THE BODY.

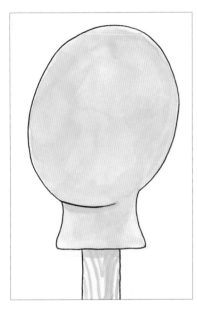

1. (**Above**) Make a simple armature (page 64) and cover it with a layer of your chosen modeling material. Add pads to the top and bottom to make an egg-shaped oval. A young child has less on the chin than an adult. Take time to practice making a perfectly smooth form at this stage, viewing it from all sides, top and bottom, removing or adding more material as necessary. Wrap clay around the neck and blend it smoothly into the head.

2. (**Right**) Mark the features on the front of the head. Use a needle to lightly score a vertical line down the center of the face, followed by a central horizontal line. For an adult, this will be the line that the eyes lie on. Score another line halfway down the lower half of the face to mark the tip of the nose. Press in the eye sockets with your fingers; then add a nose shape, two round pads for the cheeks, and a little more on the chin. Blend and smooth the surface.

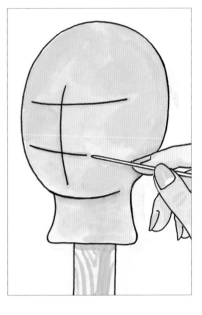

3. (**Below**) Ears extend from a line level with the eyebrows down to a line that is level with the bottom of the nose. However, they are not necessary for a female with long hair. The diagrams show where to position them for young children and adults.

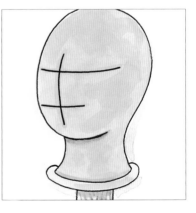

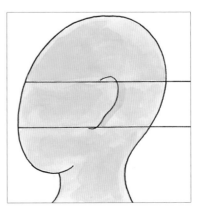

4. (**Above**) Finish the neck by adding a collar of clay around the bottom edge and building out a flange that will keep the head securely inside the body skin. A groove can be added for additional security.

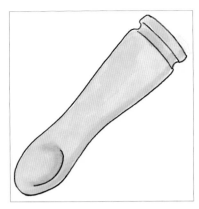

Head, and lower arms and simple boot legs, made originally in natural clay and here reproduced in porcelain.

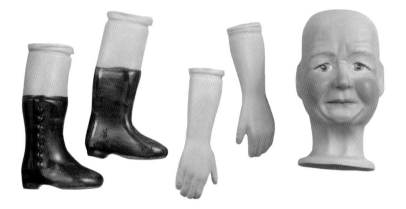

5. (Above) Take two equal-sized rolls of clay for the arms and slightly flatten one end on each. Round off and shape the flattened ends to make old-fashioned spoon hands. Then smooth the surface and at the other end of the arms, score a deep groove with a knitting needle. Fingers can be lightly scored, and a thumb can be made by cutting out a wedge on the side with scissors. Keep it simple to begin with.

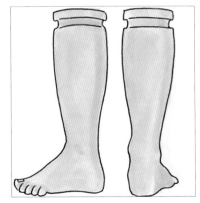

6. (Above) Since most feet are covered by socks and shoes, all you need is two rolls of clay, roughly bent and shaped as feet without toes. Concentrate on shaping ankles and insteps, and finish with grooves at the top for attaching to cloth upper legs.

7. Dry or cure all pieces, sand surfaces smooth as necessary, and paint.

Lorna Hennessey's Shepherd showing close up detail of the modeling for the head and hands and embroidery for the traditional, Hampshire smock.

sculpting a character doll

THE FOLLOWING INSTRUCTIONS DESCRIBE IN SOME DETAIL THE STEPS FOR SCULPTING A HEAD AND ARMS WITH SUPER SCULPEY. THIS PARTICULAR CLAY IS ECONOMICAL AND EASY TO USE WHEN WORKED OVER AN ARMATURE. ITS FLESH TONE, WHICH DARKENS SLIGHTLY WHEN CURED, HAS A MATTE FINISH THAT IS PERFECT FOR PAINTING WITH ACRYLICS.

Any of the other oven-curing clays (see page 25) can be substituted, but note that they will behave in their own characteristic way and may need different temperatures for curing. The order of work stays the same.

A 1 lb (453.59g) box of Super Sculpey is enough to make a head and hands for a doll the size of Hannah or Santa Claus (see pages 116 and 119). In addition, you will need four short lengths of dowel for the arms, two of which should be set upright on a base board, and another base board with a single dowel set in it for the head armature. The thickness of the dowel should match the size of doll being made. In this instance a diameter of ⅜ in (8mm) is sufficient. Aluminum foil, modeling tools, a glass rolling pin and a tile to roll on, a pair of eyes, and a cardboard tube from a roll of paper towels complete the list of materials.

1. Set up the armature for the head by preparing a length of cardboard for the shoulders and impaling it on the dowel. Add a foil collar for the neck and a crumpled ball of foil for the head. Use more crushed foil to wrap around the shoulders and head to hold it all together. Keep rotating the head as you work to get a good basic shape, adding foil as necessary. Pack foil under the cardboard shoulder for support and finally cover the entire armature with a single smooth layer of foil. This will make it easier to remove the armature from the completed sculpture.

English peddler designed by Lesley Roberts and interpreted here by Sylvia Critcher. The original sculpture was made in water clay, then used to produce a mold from which dolls could be made in various casting slips.

2. (Above) Super Sculpey is packed in four layers. Knead the top layer until it is soft and pliable. Using small amounts at a time, roll out thin layers and overlay them on the head, covering the foil armature completely.

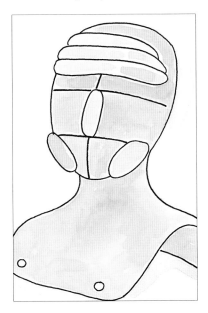

3. (Above) Add more clay to the basic shape, building up the head in rough layers. Score the position of the nose, eyes, and mouth. Create a jawline by adding a triangular piece of clay on each side of the face, make the nose with a thin long rectangle, and put flattened coils across the forehead.

4. (Above) Turn the head as you work, observing it from all directions and adding clay as necessary to build the shape. Push in eye sockets below the eyebrows. Now add clay to the neck and shoulders, extending down to shape the shoulder plate. Make holes for attaching the shoulders to the body. At this stage you are simply making a basic head shape with a rather bland surface.

5. Place the head, complete with the armature, in the oven and cure for 15 to 20 minutes, checking frequently. The clay will darken and you can test by pressing your fingernail onto the cooled surface. A properly cured head should neither indent nor leave any marks on the surface. Prepare the second layer of Super Sculpey from the box, and using very small amounts, smear a film over the surface, pushing it firmly against the cured base. If any of the following stages is less than satisfactory, the clay can simply be removed, which will always bring you back to this point, ready to start the finer detailing again.

6. (Right) If the eyes have stalks, gently pry them apart by inserting a knife in the seam line and twisting. Ideally, you should embed a spare eye into some clay and test both in the oven to check compatibility and to make sure the eye is heatproof and will not crack.

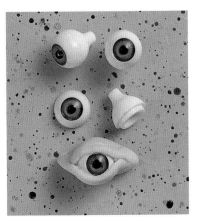

7. (Right) Put pads of clay in the eye sockets and press the eyes in place. Now roll out coils of clay and position them as eyelids, upper and lower lips, forehead, and inside cheeks next to the mouth. Then make balls of various sizes and position on the end of the nose, nostrils, upper cheeks, and chin. Finally make ovals for basic ear shapes and press in place.

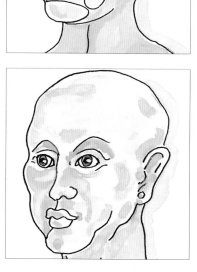

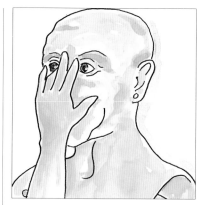

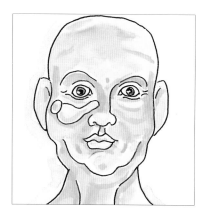

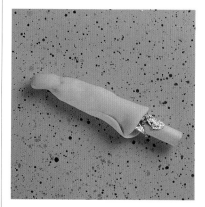

8. Working from the eyes up to the forehead, smooth and blend all the clay together to form the features in greater detail. View your work from all angles and add more clay as necessary. Continue blending, working down the nose and across the face into the mouth. The head can now become male or female, happy or sad, as it takes on an identity. Observe people closely or work with photographs for inspiration. Working in this way, adding small pieces of clay gradually, allows greater control of your sculpture.

Finish shaping and smoothing the mouth and nostrils and add details of creases and wrinkles to suit the character. These can include furrows on the forehead, wrinkles at the corner of the eyes, creases formed by smiling, and lines indicating age. Move down to the neck, adding detail to enhance the character.

9. Sculpt ear details and make holes for earrings if you wish. Make a final check of your sculpture, including looking at it in a mirror and down on the head from above. When you are satisfied that everything is in place, cure for 15 to 20 minutes and leave to cool before taking it off the stand and removing all the foil.

10. (Above) Measure the head from the chin to the top of forehead; this is the length of the hand from the tip of middle finger down to the wrist, while the width will be half the width of the face. Remember that the hands should be smaller than the measurements indicate so that they appear more in scale. It is also advisable to prepare them at the same time. making a pair.

11. (Above) Using the third layer of Super Sculpey from the box, knead it until soft and smooth, then divide it in half, one piece for each hand, and proceed as follows. Take a small quantity and roll out a ⅛-in (3mm) thick sheet and wrap it around a foil-covered dowel. Close one end of the clay to make a small fist, leaving the other end open to expose a short length of dowel.

12. Make the second lower arm in the same way, place both on a metal plate, and cure for 15 to 20 minutes with the armature left in place throughout for strength and support. These are the basic working shapes to which detail is added later.

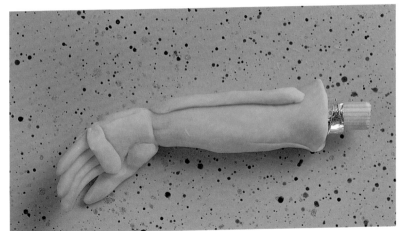

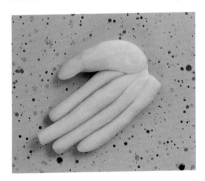

13. **(Above)** Roll out a small piece of clay into a long thin sausage and cut into eight. Choose pieces for middle fingers that are right for the length of hand required. Add fingers on each side, checking your own hand for correct proportions. Shape additional elongated triangular pieces for thumbs and add them to fingers. Make sure you have made a right and left hand.

15. **(Above)** Add a flat piece of clay to the insides of the hands covering the palms, the rolls across the base of the fingers, and the pads at the bottom of the thumbs. Smooth them together, then pose the fingers and thumbs. Finally, add a long roll down each side of the arms from wrist to elbow. Shape and blend, then finish by working details on fingers, lines on hands, and creases around the wrists.

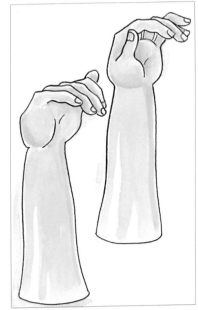

16. **(Left)** Remove the dowels from the foil. Place each arm upright on the armature rack and cure in the oven for approximately 15 minutes, checking every three minutes to monitor progress as fingers are easily scorched. Remove from the rack and withdraw the foil when the clay has cooled.

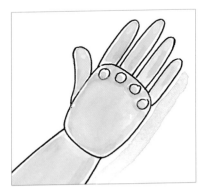

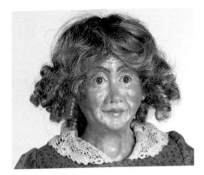

14. **(Above)** Return to the basic working shapes and smear a small amount of clay over the fists, shaping curved or straight palms. Add fingers and a flat piece of clay over the back of each hand, building up the shape. Then apply small balls of clay for the knuckles and smooth it all together.

17. **(Above right)** Super Sculpey is such a good Caucasian skin color that very little painting is needed, especially if false eyelashes are used on the upper eyelids. Paint lips and fingernails with a base of Venetian red, raw sienna, and white with a touch of cadmium red, a soft color that can also be pounced on for cheeks. Darken the base color by adding a little cerulean blue and black and use it to enhance sculptured depths on the neck, eye sockets, and the side of the nose. Eyebrows should be painted to match wigs.

Dolls
to make

The following projects have all been carefully designed to illustrate how different techniques can be successfully combined to make an exciting collection of dolls. It is a progressive series starting with simple sewn play dolls made from patterns which leads to sculpting original characters and minature dressmaking, both of which are a challenge for any dollmaker.

simple starter dolls

THE SIMPLEST POSSIBLE DOLLS CAN BE MADE FROM A SINGLE SHAPE: A PILLOW DOLL HAS A BASIC BLOCK SHAPE: RECTANGULAR AS PILLOWS USUALLY ARE, TRIANGULAR, ROUND, OR EVEN A RECTANGLE WITH AN ARCHED TOP. THE FACE, CLOTHING, ARMS, AND LEGS CAN BE DRAWN, EMBROIDERED, PAINTED, APPLIQUÉD, OR STITCHED ON. SEMICIRCLES CAN BE ADDED FOR FEET, AND ARMS CAN BE EITHER SEPARATE LITTLE PILLOWS OR REPRESENTED WITH APPLIQUÉ OR TRAPUNTO TECHNIQUES (SEE BELOW). HAIR CAN BE STITCHED OR PAINTED, OR MADE BY ATTACHING FABRIC OR YARN.

Many variations are possible: experiment with other shapes or design different costumes for the dolls shown here. Put together a patchwork fabric and make it into a pillow, then add a face and hair.

TRAPUNTO

Trapunto is a technique in which fabric, such as the arms on the pillow doll here, is applied to the base fabric. A tiny slit is made in the lower fabric, and small quantities of stuffing are pushed in from behind to give a raised effect. Stitch the slit carefully afterward.

MATERIALS NEEDED FOR THE DOLLS

Scraps of fabric

Lengths of yarn

Embroidery thread, lace, and other trimmings

Fabric paints or waterproof colored pens

Fiberfill for stuffing

Sewing thread and needle

Thin cardboard

Acrylic paints

Paint brush

TRIANGULAR PILLOW DOLL

The triangular doll is made in white satin with a more elaborately decorated dress, yarn hair, and face and arms attached separately. Trace the patterns onto paper, drawing a whole triangle for the body.

1 BODY AND SLEEVES (Right)
Fold a piece of fabric right sides together, and mark the body pattern and a pair of sleeves on it. Stitch the body and sleeves along the marked lines, leaving an opening on the lower edge of the body and on the wrists for turning and stuffing. Cut out, adding ¼ in (6mm) seam allowances all around. Mark and cut a pair of hands in flesh-colored felt.

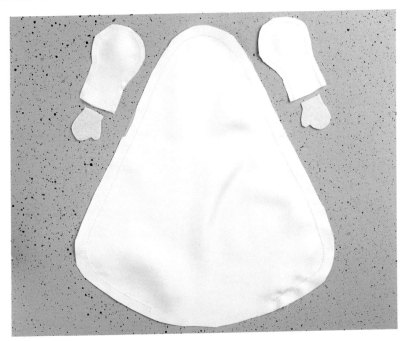

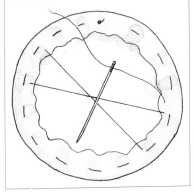

2 FACE
Cut the smaller face circle from thick nonwoven interfacing, or thin cardboard and the larger face circle in flesh-colored woven fabric. Trace the face features lightly in pencil on the fabric, and then draw them with waterproof pens: brown lines, blue or green eyes, and red mouth. Make a black dot for the pupils. With acrylic paint, make white dots for the eye highlights. Alternatively, use fabric paints in the same colors. Run a row of gathering stitch near the edge of the fabric circle.

3
Turn the body and hands right side out. Stuff the body firmly, close the opening. Stuff the sleeves more flatly and turn up hems on the wrist edges. Slip the felt hands in each sleeve, thumbs inward, and attach with blind stitching (invisible stitch). Place the face fabric over the stiff circle, and pull the gathers at the back; adjust so the face is centered on the circle. Pull the gathers firmly and stitch across the opening to secure.

4
Decorate the dress as you wish. Raid your trimmings box and be creative. We have stitched several rows of colored cotton lace around the body. Slipstitch the face to the top corner of the triangular body, about ¼ in (6mm) from the edges. Pin the arms to the body and stitch in place. Wind lengths of yarn into curls to frame the face. Finish with a bow under her chin.

MAKING THE RECTANGULAR PILLOW DOLL

Our second starter doll is a child-like rectangular doll, with embroidered face, fabric hair, trapunto arms, and separate feet.

1 **BODY** Cut three rectangles of fabric. You need one for the face, in muslin (calico) or flesh-colored cotton fabric, 9 × 3 in (23 × 7.5cm); one for the shirt in checked, striped, or print fabric, 9 × 3 in (23 × 7.5cm), and one for the pants (trousers) in plain fabric 9 × 4 in (23 × 10cm).

With right sides together, stitch them along the long edges with the patterned fabric in the middle to form a 9 in (23cm) square. Press seams to one side.

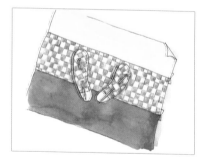

2 **ARMS** Cut a pair of arms from shirt fabric, and a pair of hands from face fabric. Stitch one hand to each wrist. Mark a point along the face/shirt seam, 2½ in (6.3cm) from each side edge, and pin arms to the body as shown, top of arm just below marked point. Attach arms to body, first with a straight stitch very near the

edge to secure in place, then with satin stitch; go around hands and wrists as well. Carefully cut tiny slits on the fabric underneath both arms and hands, and insert small amounts of stuffing inside. Close slits.

3 With right sides together, pin and stitch the sides of the rectangle to make the back seam; press seam open and refold so it is at center back.

4 **HAIR** Cut three 4 in (10cm) squares in a suitable color, and place them on top of each other. Mark 1¼ in (32mm) from one edge, and fold along this line. Insert the hair fabric, folded edge uppermost, and long side toward the back seam, in the head opening of the doll, so the folded edge is visible and lines up with raw edges. Stitch twice through all layers with a ¼ in (6mm) seam.

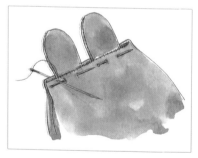

5 **FEET** Turn body right side out. Make a pair of double feet in pants fabric by stitching the curved edges, turn them right side out. Stuff the body well and the feet lightly. Turn the raw edges of the body under evenly; attach the feet to hide the raw edges and slipstitch to close.

6 Cut strips on the hair fabric, back and front. Mark the face with two dots for the eyes and a curved line for the mouth. Embroider the eyes with satin stitch in brown, and the mouth with stem stitch in red or pink.

basic cloth doll

THIS MODERN VERSION OF A TRADITIONAL RAG DOLL STANDING 17 IN (43CM) TALL INTRODUCES ALL THE BASIC SKILLS NEEDED TO MAKE AND DRESS A DOLL. THE LEGS HAVE A SIMPLE HINGE JOINT, WHILE THE HEAD IS DESIGNED WITH A THREE-DIMENSIONAL CHIN AND A FACE DRAWN WITH FINE-LINE FABRIC PENS.

MATERIALS NEEDED FOR THE DOLL

12 x 45 in (30.5 x 115cm)-wide muslin (calico)

12 x 18 in (30.5 x 46cm) printed cotton for legs

6 oz (170g) stuffing

2 oz (56g) worsted yarn (double knitting wool) for hair

Brown, black, and red waterproof pens

Powder blush for cheeks and eyes

White paint for eye highlights

MATERIALS NEEDED FOR THE CLOTHES

8 x 36 in (20 x 92cm)-wide white cotton lawn for petticoat and panties

1 yd (92cm) narrow lace to trim underwear

12 in (30.5cm) narrow elastic for panties

12 x 45 in (30.5 x 115cm)-wide printed cotton

2 snaps (press studs)

1 yd (92cm) lace to trim dress

1 yd (92cm) bias strip

MAKING THE DOLL

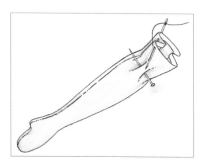 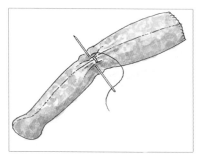 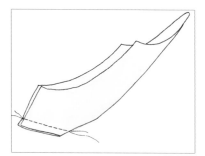

1 **ARMS** Sew arms leaving straight edges open, clip curves, turn right side out and stuff firmly to about 1¼ in (32mm) from opening. Secure with a long pin. Fold raw edges in and pleat sides to reduce width. Whip edges together and set aside.

2 **LEGS** As arms but before pinning, press tops flat bringing seams to center. Fold in raw edges of each leg in turn, whip together. Remove pins and at the knee, work a gap in the stuffing. Sew a few long stitches across to make a permanent knee joint.

3 **BODY** Sew dart on back body by bringing B to B and sewing A to B, then sew back to front, leaving lower edge open. Clip curves and turn right side out. Topstitch across neck tab and stuff body firmly. Close opening and set aside.

ASSEMBLING THE DOLL

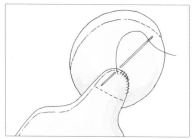 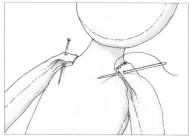

4 **HEAD** Sew head pieces together, trim seam, and turn right side out. Finger press seam by running thumb along the inside, flattening and stretching it. Now stuff head, molding as you work. Be critical and if you are not entirely happy, make again. Close opening, pulling up as you work to draw the sides in.

5 Place leg with inside leg at center front. Now turn so toes face the neck and whip together at back with strong thread. Repeat for second leg. Position head on body, sew neck tab to head, then stuff neck. Ladder stitch between the neck and back of chin.

6 Pin each arm in turn across shoulder seam, about ¾ in (18mm) back from the corner so they lie flat. Make sure they are paired, with thumbs facing forward and level with top of legs. Sew in place and remove pins.

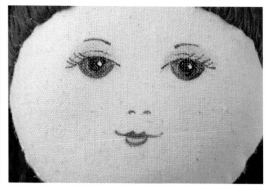

7 Draw a freestyle face on doll or trace the features given on the pattern grid and work following the sequence outlined on pages 38–39.

MAKING THE HAIR

8 Cut 34 strands of yarn each 12 in (30.5cm) long. Backstitch to top of head in front of seam hanging down to cover face. Now cut 34 strands 14 in (35.5cm) long and backstitch in place on the crown so they hang down the back. Finally cut two sets of 16 strands, each 12 in (30.5cm) long and sew a set on to each side of the head.

9 Tie a length of yarn around the hairline, making sure it covers the neck tab at the back. Lift the strands to expose face and adjust as necessary. Backstitch yarn along the hairline.

10 Unravel each strand to produce softly-waved fibers. Finger comb strands to lie straight, then gather on top of head and tie a pony tail. Finally cut 17 strands 7 in (18cm) long and tie together in the center. Unravel and sew as bangs (fringe) halfway between forehead and crown. Trim uneven ends.

MAKING THE CLOTHES

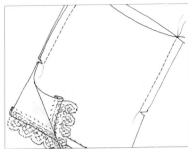

11 **PANTIES** Hem a short edge of each panty piece and apply lace. Place right sides together and sew down 4½ in (11.5cm) from the waist on each side to make center front and back seams. Clip seams at this point, press open. Refold to make separate legs and sew inside leg seam. Make a casing at the waist for elastic.

13 Gather waist edge of skirt to fit bodice. Spread gathers evenly and sew. Press under a narrow single fold from neck to hem on both sides. Fold bias strip in half lengthwise, sew to neck edge. Trim and clip seam allowance. Turn bias up, then fold over back edges of dress and sew.

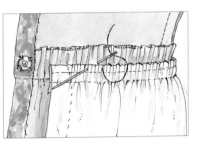

15 **PETTICOAT** Hem short sides and one long edge. Trim long edge with lace. Fold down ½ in (12mm) at waist and gather until it is just slightly narrower than the waist. Distribute fullness evenly, then slipstitch the petticoat to the waist seam of the dress.

12 **DRESS** Sew bodice front and backs together at shoulders, press seams open. Gather cap (head) of each sleeve, pull up to fit armhole opening. Match centers, adjust gathers, then sew each sleeve in place. Trim seams and clip curves. Hem wrist edge. Fold bodice right sides together and sew each side in turn from wrist, up arm, down side to waist.

14 Turn bias to inside and hem to neck seam. Sew snaps (press studs) at neck and waist. Hem lower edge of dress and trim with lace around the skirt and bodice, suggesting a square yoke.

lavinia

STANDING 22½ IN (57CM) TALL, LAVINIA IS A FULLY FASHIONED CLOTH DOLL WITH ADULT PROPORTIONS, INNOVATIVE KNEE JOINTS, AND A FLAT FACE WHICH IS A PERFECT CANVAS FOR EMBROIDERED FEATURES. SHE IS DRESSED AS A 1920s FLAPPER IN LONG EVENING WEAR TOGETHER WITH COMPLEMENTARY ACCESSORIES.

MATERIALS NEEDED FOR THE DOLL

½ yd x 45 in (50 x 115cm)-wide muslin (calico)

10 oz (290g) stuffing

½ yd x 3 in (50 x 7.5cm)-deep hair-colored fringe

Six-strand embroidery threads for working the face

Color pencils for shading lips and eyes

Powder blush for cheeks

Plastic plant labels, or strips of plastic cut from a food container measuring ¾ x 5 in (18mm x 13cm), rounded at one end and straight at the other

MATERIALS NEEDED FOR THE CLOTHES

½ yd x 45 in (50 x 115cm)-wide silk satin for underclothes

10 x 45 in (25 x 115cm)-wide sheer silk for dress

10 x 45 in (25 x 115cm)-wide shot silk for wrap

14 x 16 in (35.5 x 40cm) silk for turban

Narrow braid to make straps for dress

12 in (30.5cm) narrow elastic

24 x 1 in (60cm x 25mm)-wide lace

1 yd (92m) ruffle trim for wrap

3 snap fasteners (press studs)

Feathers, beads, ribbon roses, or ruffles to trim turban

Silver Glitter fabric paint for slippers

Narrow silver cord to trim slippers

Pearl necklace

MAKING THE DOLL

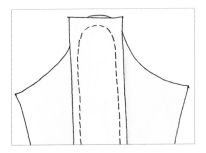

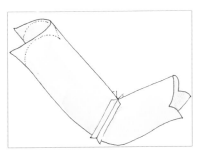

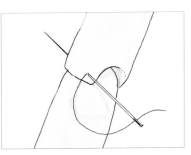

1 Lay armature pocket on wrong side of the body back and sew in place, leaving the bottom open. Trim excess pocket from neck edge. Complete back by sewing darts, slit open, and press flat. Fold up lower edge by ¼ in (6mm) and press.

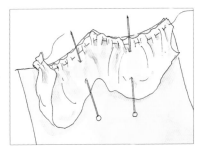

2 Assemble body front, sewing sections together in the following order: Gather lower edge of chest, pull up and press gathers, then sew to lower front from B to A on one side, then B to A on the other. Clip B on lower front first to ease tension. Now sew neck to chest from C to D on each side in turn. Do not sew straight across. Clip seams to ease tension.

3 Sew front and back together across shoulders, then down each side from E to G. Turn up lower edge and press. Clip curves and turn right side out. Insert plastic strips in armature pocket, then stuff body firmly, molding it into shape as you work. Close lower edge, catching together at H. Close each side in turn, inserting more stuffing as needed and pulling up slightly to draw sides inward.

4 Sew foot to lower leg J–K–J and clip seam. Then fold leg lengthwise matching ankle seams and sew L–J–M. Press foot flat, bringing Ms and N together, then sew across toes. Now shape knee by sewing O–P and Q–R, cutting last dart open. Trim both curves, then refold leg bringing P and Q together. Complete the "ball" joint of knee by sewing from S through P–Q to S. Trim curve, turn right side out, stuff firmly, and close. Make second lower leg.

5 Fold upper leg lengthwise and sew into a tube. Press seam open and refold bringing seam to center back. Then sew across bottom opening in a curve, matching S–P–Q–S of lower leg.

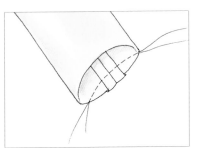

6 Now turn curved end inward to form the cup of the "socket" joint. Check that the knee fits in the cup. If it is too tight, it will not work. For the knee to bend, you must curve the back edge by sewing across the back seam. The horizontal front edge will act as a stop, preventing lower leg from bending forward. Turn right side out and again check.

7 Stuff firmly at the bottom, carefully preserving the cup, then less firmly at top. Turn in edges and whip together. Make second upper leg. Position each knee in turn in the corresponding socket and sew together from side to side with strong thread.

8 The arms have a false ball and socket joint at the shoulders, rigid elbows, and topstitched fingers. Sew around each arm, following curves and reinforcing stitching between thumbs and fingers. Clip and trim seam and turn right side out. Stuff hand lightly, holding stuffing in place with a pin at the wrist. Topstitch fingers, remove pin, stuff arm firmly, and close opening.

9 Press both back sections of head along fold lines, then open out and place one on top of the other with folds together. Sew across fold line, leaving central section open. Fold back each section to make head shape and finish by sewing darts. Make same darts on face, then sew to back of head, leaving it open at top. Turn right side out and stuff to a firm shape with a smooth outline around the chin. Close opening.

ASSEMBLING THE DOLL

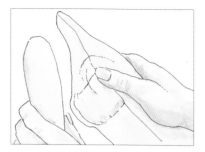

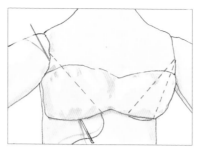

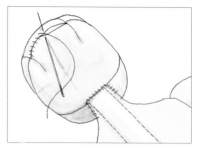

10 Push your thumb against the side of the body at E and move it back and forth till you have formed a socket under a folded ridge of fabric that the arm can be stitched to. The arm only needs to be sewn across the top, remaining free to lift up and down. Attach second arm.

11 Once the arms are in place, it is possible to shape the bust. Take a long surface stitch under each breast, pull it up, and tie off under the arm.

12 Sew legs to lower front of body with inside edges together at H.

13 Work your thumb into the head through the back opening and make a cavity to accommodate the neck. Position head on neck, then ladder stitch in place.

MAKING THE FACE AND HAIR

14 Mark eye positions with pencil spots or pins. Then using two strands, embroider each iris with stem stitch, pupils and highlights with straight stitch, and eye outline with stem stitch. Work eyelashes with a single strand. Complete both eyes before embroidering straight stitch nostrils and stem stitch mouth. Finish with stem stitch eyebrows.

15 Use color pencils to shade in eye shadow and color the lips. Then use powder blush to color the cheeks.

16 Cut a length of fringe to pass around back of head from ear to ear and sew in place. Cut a shorter length to sit on the front of the head and position it so that the fringe just touches the eyes. Sew in place.

MAKING THE CLOTHES

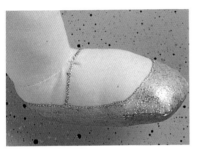

17 Paint slippers onto feet. Whe they are dry, couch silver cord around edge of each slipper and then across the foot to make narrow straps.

18 Assemble panties with French seams at center front and back, followed by inside legs. Fold down waist edge and sew a casing for the elastic. Insert elastic to fit join ends, then close. Trim legs with lace.

19 Join bodice front and back of slip on the right-hand side with a French seam. Now prepare right-hand hip dart by gathering between the dots and pulling up to fit slash at bottom of bodice. Fold ungathered portion into an inverted pleat. Match bodice seam to center of pleat. With raw edges even, sew across.

20 Gather each lower edge of hip darts on left-hand side of dress in turn, pull up to fit slash, and sew. There are no pleats with these darts. Hem long side openings of slip, followed by deeper hem across the top of bodice and lower edge. Finish slip by sewing snaps (press studs) between hip and armpit.

21 The dress front and back are both prepared in the same way. Make a ½ in (12mm) right angle cut to the edge on both long sides of the front and back, 5 in (13cm) back from a short end. This separates the main fall of the dress from a shorter flap that folds down from the top.

22 Hem short flaps to one side and main fall of dress to the other. Fold down flaps, then catch to slip with the shoulder straps, which are made from narrow braid. Do this on both front and back, making sure the dress and slip will fit over the head. Gather excess width of the dress at the top on each side in turn and catch to slip under the arms. Leaving flaps to hang free, catch sides of dress to slip at hips.

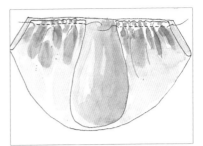

23 Make wrap by gathering between A and B and pull up until A to B plus C fits the shoulder seam A to C. Repeat on other side. Narrow hem all raw edges. Trim wrap with ruffle, joining ends at center back.

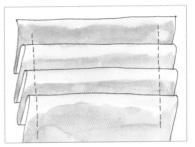

24 Pleat long width of turban into three upward-facing folds, reducing depth to 8 in (20cm). Sew folds down on one side, then 3½ in (9cm) in from the other edge. Seam long edges together making a tube. Turn right side out and gather the end where folds are already stitched down. Wrap turban around head, crossing ends over in the front and tuck loose end in at the top. Stitch turban together, decorating the crossover with a trim.

(Left) The Pirate by English doll artist, Lesley Roberts. A wonderful needle sculptured character that is presented complete with felt parrot, carved wooden stump and crutch, base board, and suitably charred treasure map.

(Right) Amish Doll made by the author from a pattern based on an antique original. These dolls are distinguished by their lack of facial features and the plain-colored fabrics used for their costumes. The colors are traditionally from one half of the color wheel, red-violet to green which is offset with black.

stretch jersey doll

THIS 16 IN (40CM) TALL CHARACTER DOLL HAS A NEEDLE-SCULPTED HEAD MADE AS SHOWN IN "NEEDLE SCULPTURE," IN THE TECHNIQUES SECTION OF *MAKING A START*. THE ARMS AND LEGS ARE ALSO MADE IN STRETCH JERSEY AND NEEDLE SCULPTED, BUT THE BODY IS WOVEN COTTON FABRIC AND FORMS PART OF THE CLOTHING, WHICH IS MOSTLY NOT REMOVABLE. LIMBS ARE JOINED TO THE BODY WITH BUTTONS AND STRONG THREAD. THE HAIR IS MADE IN FANTASY COLORS FROM SPACE-DYED SLUB YARN, BUT ANY SUITABLE HAIR MATERIAL CAN BE USED (SEE PAGES 22-23).

PROJECT

MATERIALS NEEDED FOR THE DOLL AND CLOTHES

11 x 28 in (28 x 71cm) flesh-colored jersey or stockinette fabric for head, arms, and legs

8 x 9 in (20 x 23cm) woven cotton fabric for body

7½ x 20 in (19 x 51cm) fabric for skirt

11 x 12 in (28 x 30.5cm) fabric for sleeves and waistband

12 x 15 in (30.5 x 38cm) fabric for vest (waistcoat) and boots

7 x 10 in (18 x 25cm) fabric for vest lining (can be the same as for skirt)

8 x 12 in (20 x 30.5cm) fabric for boots lining (can be the same as for body)

4 oz (112g) polyester stuffing

30 x 1 in (76cm x 25mm)-wide cotton lace

2¼ yd (2m) very narrow ribbon

1 oz (28g) yarn for hair

White quilting thread

Four flat ⅝ in (15mm) diameter buttons, preferably with only two holes

Strong carpet thread

Fine long needle for needle-sculpting (No. 7 darning needle is ideal)

Toy needle at least 5 in (13cm) long for jointing limbs

Brown waterproof and fadeproof fine-nib pen

Acrylic fabric paints in blue, red, white, black, brown

Glitter paint for eye shadow

A fine paint brush, suitable for acrylics

MAKING THE DOLL

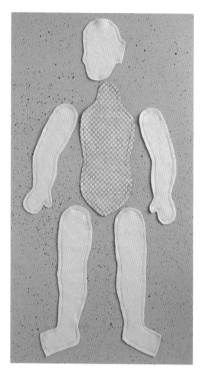

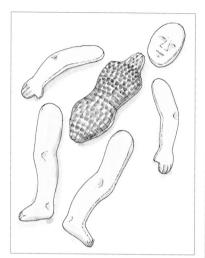

1 Prepare the patterns by copying them on cardboard. Trace one face, two arms, and two legs on the folded jersey fabric, leaving enough space between the pieces to add ¼ in (6mm) seam allowances. Pin the two layers of fabric together. Do not cut yet. Machine stitch the pieces on the marked lines, leaving openings where indicated. Mark one body on the folded body fabric, pin and machine stitch as before. Cut all the pieces out, adding seam allowances of ¼ in (6mm) around all the seams.

2 Take the legs, and pinch the toe area across, so that the seams are brought together in the center. Pin them together, and draw a round foot shape on the fabric for the toe seam, and machine stitch it. Trim corners. Turn all the pieces right side out.

3 Stuff all the pieces. The head, arms, and legs should be shaped and molded so the fabric does not stretch excessively. Close all the openings with ladder stitch. Needle-sculpt hands, elbows, feet, ankles, and knees as shown on page 57 in "Needle Sculpture."

4 Needle-sculpt and paint the head as described in "Needle Sculpture." First needle-sculpt the nose; then paint the eyes and mouth; finally needle-sculpt the eyes and mouth.

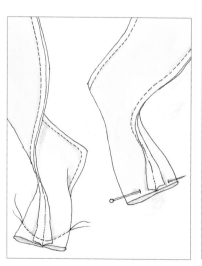

ASSEMBLING THE DOLL

5 Join the limbs to the body with buttons and strong thread. Push the needle first through one leg, then through the body, then out through the other leg. Use a pair of pliers to pull the needle out if necessary. Cut off the thread close to the needle eye, leaving thread ends the same length on each side.

Slip each thread strand through a hole in the button, on both sides. Tie a knot to hold the button in, and pull the thread evenly from both sides to tighten the legs to the body. Make a second knot, and then pull the threads under the button and around the shaft, tying them two or three time; cut tails off. Repeat for the arms.

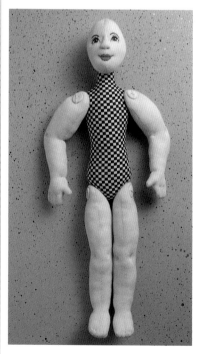

6 Place the head on the body, fitting the shaped lower back of the head onto the neck. Hold with pins, and ladder stitch all around, leaving a chin at the front.

MAKING THE CLOTHES

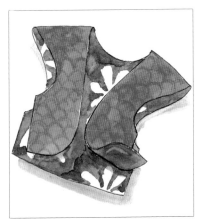

10 BOOTS Place the two fabrics, top and lining, right sides together, and mark the boot pattern twice on them. Stitch along the top area only, from one toe to the other. Cut out, adding seam allowances to the stitched top seam. Trim corners and snip curves, and turn right side out. Press. With boot side out, overlap the two finished edges of the top side and stitch. Turn again, lining side out; pin lower seams to form sole, all four layers together, and stitch. Pinch the toe area as for foot, and stitch with curved seam as for toes. Trim and turn right side out. Put on doll, turning points out for lining to show.

7 SLEEVES Cut a strip 2½ x 7 in (6.3 x 18cm) for the waistband, then cut two sleeves. Turn under a narrow hem on the bottom edges and attach lace. Run a gathering stitch along the curved edges. Fold each sleeve right sides together and stitch the short sides. Pull the gathers and slip the sleeves onto the doll's shoulders; attach firmly.

9 VEST (WAISTCOAT) Cut two pieces of fabric one for the right side and one for the lining. Place them right sides together and mark the pattern; stitch all around, leaving an opening in the center of the straight side. Cut out, adding a ¼ in (6mm) seam allowance. Trim corners and snip curves; turn right side out, pushing corners out with a pencil. Press and close back seam. Try on doll, overlap sides, pin and stitch in place.

11 FINISHING DETAILS. Wrap narrow ribbon around the neck and make a bow with long tail ends. Wrap around one wrist and knot; and wrap around the boots and make a bow.

MAKING THE HAIR

8 SKIRT Turn up long edge of the fabric and attach lace. Stitch the two short edges together. Run a gathering stitch along the second long edge, pull up gathers, and put on the doll. Tighten the waist. Fold waistband lengthwise and place on waist to cover skirt gathers; join at the back and stitch in place.

12 Wind yarn to a length of about 19 in (48cm), and about 2 in (5cm) wide when laid flat on the table. Starting at the back, secure one end of wound yarn to the back, and then take it around one side, over the top, down the other side, and up the back again. Leave enough of the last end to form a sort of bun on top of the head. Try out the arrangement first; once you are happy with it, secure it with pins and then stitch or glue to the head.

felt doll

THIS DOLL FOLLOWS THE TRADITION OF FELT
DOLLS OF THE EARLY PART OF THE TWENTIETH
CENTURY. THE PRODUCTION OF WOOL FELT
WAS A BIG INDUSTRY, AND BEAUTIFUL DOLLS
WERE MADE FROM IT, OFTEN WITH DRESSES
AND ACCESSORIES IN THE SAME MATERIAL.

MATERIALS NEEDED FOR THE DOLL

14 x 16 in (35.5 x 40cm)
unbleached muslin (calico) for the
body

11 x 16 in (28 x 40cm) flesh-
colored wool felt for arms and
legs. (If wool is not available, line
ordinary felt with iron-on
interfacing to make it strong
enough.)

7 x 8 in (18 x 20cm) wool felt in
the same color for the head

7 x 8 in (18 x 20cm) cheesecloth
(butter muslin) or buckram

4 plastic doll or teddy bear joints,
1⅜ in (35mm) size

4 x 11 in (10 x 28cm) long-haired
artificial fur fabric for hair.
(Alternatively, use a purchased
doll wig.)

8 oz (230g) polyester stuffing

3 pipecleaners or chenille stems
(optional)

3¼ in (8cm) head shape to make
the mask (measured from top of
head to chin)

White craft glue (PVA) and an
old brush

Acrylic or fabric paints in blue,
red, brown, white, and black and
a fine paint brush

Liquid detergent or petroleum
jelly

MATERIALS NEEDED FOR THE CLOTHES

14 x 28 in (35.5 x 71cm) bright-
colored felt for the dress

12 x 28 in (30.5 x 71cm)
contrasting felt for shoes and for
trimming dress

7 x 11 in (18 x 28cm) felt for the
panties (knickers)

Felt scraps in pink and green or
purchased flowers

A pair of purchased white doll
socks

2 pearl buttons for shoes

12 x ¾ in (30cm x 18mm)-wide
ribbon in contrasting color

The mask faces were then machine-
made, but the techniques in "Face
Masks" (on page 60), explain how to
make one by hand. This doll's body is
made of strong cotton fabric to
support the joints that allow her to
sit and to move her arms. The rest
(arms, legs, face, clothing, and
accessories) are all made from felt.
Her hair is a wig made from long fur
fabric, but she also looks good in a
purchased wig.

With the advent of manufactured
fabrics, such as nylon, wool felt is
rarer now, but it is still made and is
recommended for its strength.

MAKING THE FACE

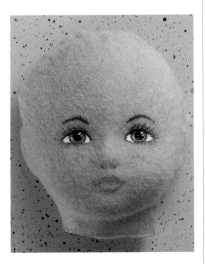

1 Make a head mask in felt, as explained on page 61–63, "Face Masks." Use a head 3¼ to 3½ in (8 to 9cm) long from top of head to chin. Make a first mask layer with cheesecloth (butter muslin) or buckram soaked in craft glue. When dry, wet the 7 Ø 8 in (18 Ø 20cm) piece of wool felt and squeeze till just damp. Apply a thick coat of glue to the first layer and make the second mask layer of felt. Leave to dry for 24 hours or more. When dry, remove from head, trim edges, and add a coat of glue on the inside of the face. When dry, paint the face as shown in "Faces" on page 38–39.

MAKING THE DOLL

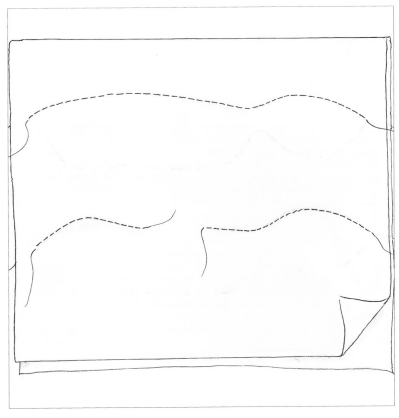

2 Prepare and cut out all the paper patterns. Fold the body fabric in half, and place the two body patterns on top. Trace around them with a pencil, marking the openings and the points for the joints; leave space between pieces for adding seam allowances. Remove the paper patterns, and machine stitch on the center front and center back marked lines. Leave an opening in the center back as shown.

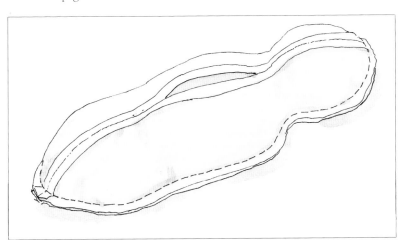

3 Cut out the two body pieces. Add a seam allowance of ¼ in (6mm) to the stitched seam and cut the rest on the line. Press the center seams open with your fingers. Place the front against the back, right sides together, matching the seams at the top of the head and the crotch. Pin and machine stitch all around, with a ¼ in (6mm) seam allowance. There is no need to leave any more openings. Clip all curves in the seams, particularly in the neck area.

4 Fold the wool felt in half, and mark two legs and two arms on it. Hold the piece together with a few pins and machine stitch all around on the marked lines, leaving openings as shown. Cut out, adding a ¼ in (6mm) seam allowance.

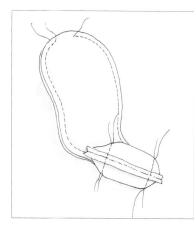

5 Form the sole of the foot by flattening the lower part of the foot so the seam stands in the middle. Pinch the front point to form a dart, and stitch across. Do the same with the back point.

6 Turn all the pieces right side out. Make the fingers by stitching three seams on each hand to form four fingers. Either stuff with tiny amounts of stuffing, or cut 1 in (25mm) pieces of pipecleaner, fold, wrap in a wisp of stuffing, and place one inside each finger and thumb. This way the hands will be more poseable.

7 Fit the plastic joints. On the inner sides of the arms and legs, transfer the positions of the joints from the paper patterns. Make a tiny hole and slip the stem of each joint through each hole. Make holes on the points of the body where the joints will go, and slip stems through them into the body. Inside the body, fit the other half of the joint (the plain circle) and secure very tightly with the washer.

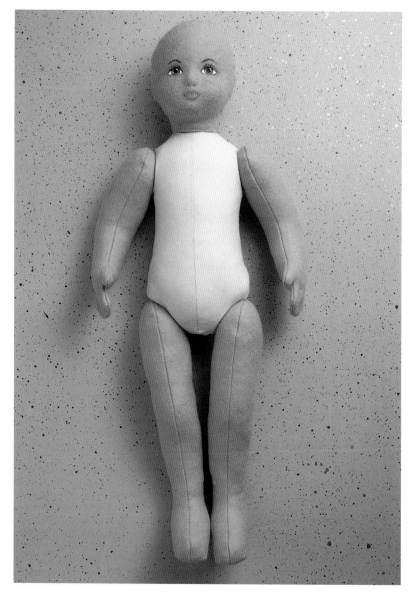

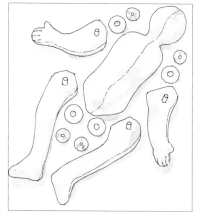

8 Stuff the body very firmly, especially the neck; the limbs can be done just a bit less hard. Close all openings with ladder stitch. Pin the face mask to the front of the head, and stitch in place.

9 Make the wig. On the fur fabric rectangle, mark 2 in (5cm) in from each end on one of the long sides. Draw a line from each mark to the corner on the other side; cut the triangles off to leave a regular trapezoid shape for the wig.

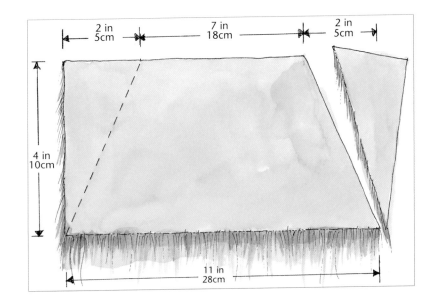

2 in
5cm

7 in
18cm

2 in
5cm

4 in
10cm

11 in
28cm

10 With right sides together, stitch the two short, now slanted, sides together. Run a gathering stitch along the shorter of the two long sides. Pull really tight to close the hole completely, and knot to hold in place. Turn right side out. Fit on the doll, and brush some of the fibers back to cover the center gathering. Trim the front to the shape of the hairline if necessary. Alternatively, use a purchased wig. Don't stitch the wig on yet, as it will be easier to try the clothes on before the wig is attached.

MAKING THE CLOTHES

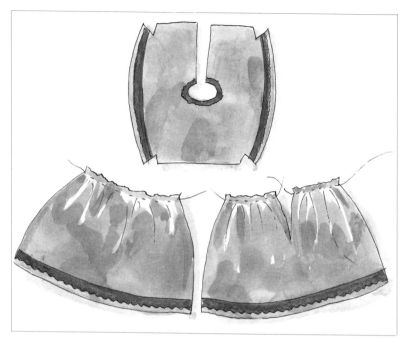

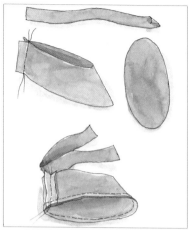

11 Prepare the patterns as indicated, making whole patterns out of half or quarter patterns when necessary. Cut one front skirt, one back skirt (which has an opening cut in the center top area), and one whole top, with a cut at the center back. Cut strips of contrasting felt, cut decorative triangles in them, and attach them to the clothes as shown. Alternatively, attach rickrack, lace, or other purchased trimmings. Run a row of gathering stitches along the waist edge of front and back skirt pieces.

14 Make the shoes. Cut two uppers from doubled felt, and stitch the back seams. Cut two soles in felt; pin and stitch to the uppers. Cut two straps, ½ in (12mm) wide by 5½ in (14cm) long, and attach the center of each strap to the shoe at the back seam. Put the socks on the doll, and try the shoes on to make sure the straps overlap at the front enough to hold the button and buttonhole. Trim if necessary. Stitch buttons and cut tiny slits for the buttonholes.

12 Pull the gathers slightly, to fit the size of the waist in the top. With right sides together, pin and stitch the front skirt to the front of the top, and the back skirt to the back of the top. With right sides together, fold the dress at the shoulders; pin and stitch the side and underarm seams. Clip underarm curves. Turn right side out. Finish dress with felt flowers (made from circles folded in half twice) or purchased ones.

13 Make the panties. Cut out one from doubled felt, and stitch the two sides. Turn right side out and put on the doll.

15 Put a ribbon bow in the doll's hair. She also looks good in a purchased straw hat.

spoon doll

THIS IS A MANNEQUIN-TYPE DOLL, 20 IN (51CM) TALL; THE SIMPLE BODY HAS NO LEGS, BUT THE BASE IS WEIGHTED TO MAKE THE DOLL FREE-STANDING. SHE HAS BEEN MADE HERE WITH THE BOWL OF A WOODEN SPOON AS A HEAD, BUT SHE CAN HAVE AN ALTERNATIVE FABRIC HEAD. THIS DOLL IS A PEG FOR THE IMAGINATION, AS THE BODY CAN BE MADE IN MANY FABRICS AND DECORATED WITH A VARIETY OF TRIMMINGS.

MATERIALS NEEDED FOR THE DOLL

Wooden spoon, bowl size about 3¾ x 2¼ in (9.5 x 5.7cm)

22 x 36in (56 x 92cm) printed fabric for body/dress

3 x 8 in (7.5 x 20cm) muslin (calico) or flesh-colored fabric for hands

4½ x 7 in (11.5 x 18cm) muslin (calico) or flesh-colored fabric for fabric head

3½ x 6 in (9 x 16cm) cardboard for base

5 yd x 1 in (4.5m x 25mm)-wide lace or eyelet (broderie anglaise)

30 in (76cm) narrow ribbon

1 yd (92cm) maribou feather trim

½ oz (14g) of mohair or other knitting yarn for hair

6 oz (170g) stuffing, ½ lb (250g) of plastic beans in a well-closed fabric bag [or a lump of modeling clay (Plasticine) of equivalent weight]

Acrylic paints in blue, red, brown, black, and white

A fine brush

Acrylic matte varnish

MAKING THE FACE

MAKING THE BODY

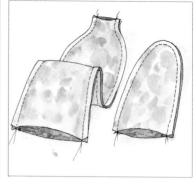

1 SPOON HEAD First give both sides of the bowl of the spoon a thin coat of acrylic varnish. Leave to dry thoroughly. Sand lightly with fine sandpaper, and wipe clean with a soft cloth. This is done to stop the paint from running on bare, unprimed wood.

Draw a face on the back, convex side of the spoon, following the face template. It can be done freehand, or cut the face template from paper and carbon paper of the same size. Center them on the spoon bowl and secure them in place with small pieces of tape on the edges. Carefully trace the main lines of the features; details such as eyelashes can be hand-drawn afterward. Remove papers and proceed to paint the face as shown on page 38–39: white for the balls of the eyes, blue for the irises, black for the pupils, white highlights; red or pink for the mouth; brown for eyelids, eyelashes, and eyebrows, and lines for the nose and center of the mouth.

2 ALTERNATIVE FABRIC HEAD Trace the outline of the head on doubled muslin (calico) or other flesh-colored cotton fabric. Stitch on the line, leaving an opening at the top. Turn right side out and stuff the head very firmly; slipstitch to close. Draw the features, either freehand in pencil, or using the face template and carbon paper as explained for the spoon head above left. Paint as above right.

3 With the body/dress fabric doubled, cut one body and two sleeves. Stitch, taking a ¼ in (6mm) seam allowance; leave the lower edges of sleeves and body and the neck open. (If you are making a fabric head, make the neck a little longer—½ in (12mm)—and do not leave it open.)

For the base, cut one oval from cardboard following the smaller, inner line, and one from fabric following the larger, outer line.

4 Turn the body right side out. Turn under ½ in (12mm) on the neck if using a spoon head. Turn under a single ¼ in (6mm) hem on the lower edge, baste (tack) in place.

Put the spoon inside the doll through the neck opening. Stuff the body very firmly, keeping the handle of the spoon centered. Place the bag of plastic beans near the bottom of the doll. Complete stuffing around it.

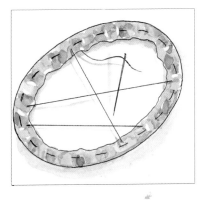

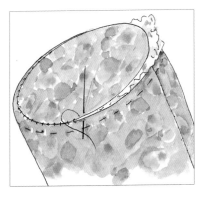

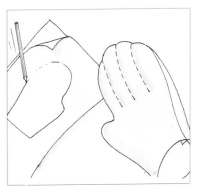

5 Run a gathering stitch ¼ in (6mm) from the edge in the fabric base. Cover the cardboard base with the fabric one, pull the gathers tightly, and secure them in place with some criss-cross stitches.

6 Pin the stiff fabric-covered base to the lower edge of the body/dress of the doll. Add more stuffing if necessary to allow the doll to stand without falling. Stitch the base in place with tiny blind stitching (invisible stitches).

7 Make a pair of hands in doubled muslin (calico), by marking the template on the fabric, stitching on the line, and cutting out. Snip between fingers and thumb, turn right side out, stuff, and stitch the fingers.

Turn the sleeves right side out, turn up a ¼ in (6mm) single hem, and attach trimming to the edge. Stuff very lightly, run a gathering row along the edge of the fabric, pull the gathers, slip a hand inside, and stitch in place.

ASSEMBLING THE DOLL

8 Make a ruffle by cutting a piece of fabric 4 Ø 36 in (10 Ø 92cm). Join the two short edges. Turn up a ¼ in (6mm) hem on one long edge, and attach lace as for arms. Turn under a ½ in (12mm) hem on the other long edge, and run a gathering stitch ¼ in (6mm) from the folded edge. Pull gathers and fit on the doll, with the lace reaching the lower edge of the body. Stitch in place.

Stitch the arms to the body as shown. Put a small piece of trimming around the neck.

9 Make the hair by winding 8 in (20cm) lengths of yarn to create enough curls to cover the back of the spoon as well. Tie up the center of the bundle lightly with a strand of the same yarn, until it is about 1 in (25mm) wide. Center it on the spoon head and arrange it to frame the edges and cover the back. When satisfied, glue hair to head. Add decorations such as ribbons, bows, feather trim, or flowers as desired.

10 If you are making a fabric head, stitch it securely to the tab neck, and make the hair as above.

11 **FINISHING DETAILS.** Wrap narrow ribbon around the neck and make a bow with long tail ends. Wrap around one wrist and knot; and wrap around the boots and make a bow.

sleepy heads

SMALL AND SIMPLE THOUGH THEY MAY APPEAR, THESE BABIES PROVIDE A WONDERFUL OPPORTUNITY TO EXPERIENCE AND EXPLORE NEEDLE SCULPTURE. THE VERY NATURE OF THEIR CREATION, AS YOU COAX FEATURES FROM THE BALL OF STUFFING, WILL MEAN THAT EACH DOLL IS A UNIQUE INDIVIDUAL. THEY MEASURE JUST 7 IN (18CM).

MATERIALS NEEDED FOR THE DOLL

These quantities will make two dolls:

9 in (23cm) square of flesh-colored stocking-knit fabric (stockinette)

Body fabric and beanbag (see Sleep suit below)

4 oz (112g) stuffing

2 oz (56g) plastic granules for beanbag

Powder blush for cheeks

Color pencils for lips and brows

MATERIALS NEEDED FOR THE CLOTHES

¼ yd (23cm) lightweight cotton for sleep suit

Pair of small bright-colored socks

Small pillows as accessories

MAKING THE DOLL

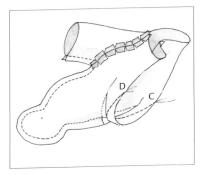

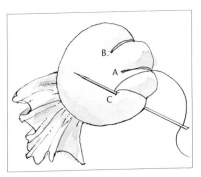

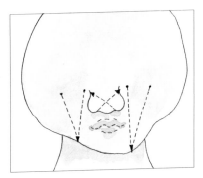

1 Make seat darts on the body back. Then sew back to front body from A to B on each side, followed by seaming from wrist to wrist around the legs. Fold body along midline, tucking one half inside the other and sew C to D. Clip corners, slash back open, and turn right side out. Stuff legs to hips.

2 Make darts on bag pieces and sew together around curved edge. Turn right side out and part-fill with granules. Gather opening, turning in raw edges, and fasten off securely. Gather each hand in turn, enclosing a little stuffing before fastening off. Sew head into a tube, then gather the top and fasten. Form a ball of stuffing the size of a golf ball in your palm and place in head. Wind thread around tube beneath stuffing to form a neck stalk. Circumference of head should be about 4 in (10cm).

3 **HAND SCULPTURE** Bring needle up at A and take thread over edge of hand. Insert needle and bring up at A again, pulling to form a crease. Take needle back over edge and bring through at B, repeat and come up at C, and so on, to make fingers. Thumbs are optional extras for babies. Make second hand to complete pair.

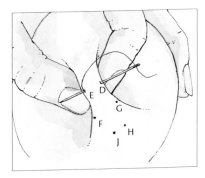

4 **HEAD SCULPTURE** Make nose quite high on face by pinching up a bridge and sewing beneath it from D to E several times, then F to G. Work side of nose by stitching in at G, out at H, and in at G, so the loop stitch lies on the surface under the bulge of the nose. Repeat on the other side from F to J. The nostrils are indented by stitches pulled from H across to F, and then from J to G.

5 Push up ridge for upper lip and stitch back and forth to hold. Then make a shorter ridge for lower lip and sew in same way. Keep surface stitches between the lips. Sleeping eyes are formed by pulling stitches downward from each corner to under the chin and locking off. These stitches also round the cheeks and make a more prominent chin.

ASSEMBLING THE DOLL

6 Position beanbag in stomach. Sew hands in sleeves with palms against the seam, then stuff arms lightly and close back opening. Sew head in place, blush cheeks, and color the lips and brows. Finally, cut a section of sock and fashion a hat, holding it in place with a stitch or two.

hannah

THIS CHALLENGING PROJECT BRINGS TOGETHER SEVERAL ASPECTS OF DOLLMAKING, FROM SCULPTING A HEAD AND HANDS, TO BUILDING A BODY AROUND A WIRE ARMATURE WHERE THERE IS NO BODY SKIN TO CONTROL THE SHAPE. COMBINE ALL THESE SKILLS TO MAKE A CHARACTER STANDING 17 IN (43CM) TALL.

MATERIALS NEEDED FOR THE DOLL

Finished shoulder head measuring 2¼ in (5.7cm) from chin to forehead

Pair of lower arms with hollow centers

5 ft (1.5m) aluminum wire

Epoxy putty

Electrical insulation tape

20 x 39 in (51 x 100cm)-wide batting (wadding)

4 oz (112g) stuffing

4 x 9in (23cm) lengths of narrow cotton tape

Ready-made wig with 7–8 in (18–20cm) head circumference

MATERIALS NEEDED FOR THE CLOTHES

Tubular waistband from a pair of panty hose

20 x 45 in (50cm x 115cm)-wide peach colored crepe de chine

24 in (61cm) lace for lower edge of petticoat

18 x 45 in (46 x 115cm)-wide cotton print

4 small buttons

Lace motif for collar

6 in (16cm) square of fleece for slippers

2 x 6 in (16cm) lengths of pipecleaner (chenille stem)

3 in (7.5cm) square of cardboard

3 in (7.5cm) square of thin leather

MAKING THE BODY

1 Set hands onto arm wire with epoxy putty and leave to set. Bend body wire in half, making a 3¼ in (8cm)-wide bridge for shoulders. Turn ends into feet 2 in (5cm) long with wires extending down to inside of each foot. Bend feet at right angles to legs; model a foot on each wire with epoxy putty. Set aside to become firm.

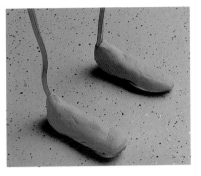

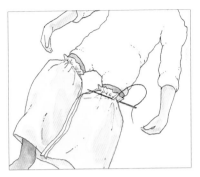

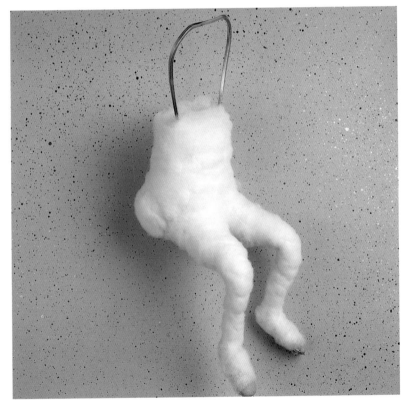

4 Cut panty hose waistband in half and gather one end of each piece. Place gathers against toes, then pull tubes up respective legs to form both stockings and leg coverings at the same time. Check shape of leg, removing stocking if necessary to make any corrections. Sew center front and back crotch of bloomers, followed by the inside leg seams. Feed onto legs inside out so that the waist is down around the ankles. Gather each leg in turn and sew onto doll through gathers and stocking beneath. Now pull bloomers up, gather waist, and sew on doll.

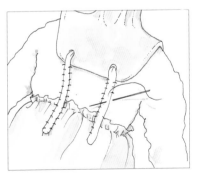

2 Wrap feet and leg wires tightly with batting and secure with long stitches. Shape calves and thighs with more wraps, stitching each strip to hold it in place and condense stuffing. Bend legs in a sitting position to form buttocks, and wrap with batting. Fill the central cavity with loose stuffing. The buttocks can be further shaped by making two separate pads and stitching them in position.

3 Bind arm wire to shoulder bridge with the tape and continue to cover wires with batting, building up the body shape and arms. Check proportions by holding shoulder with fixed head to the body, but don't attach yet.

5 Thread cotton tapes through holes in the shoulder plate and tie with secure knots. Hide knots under the shoulder plate and stitch long loops onto the body, down onto the top of the bloomers. This is more secure than sewing the head to the batting alone. The wig can be glued in place at this point, thus completing the body, or left until the doll has been dressed.

MAKING THE CLOTHES

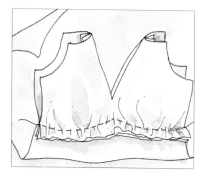

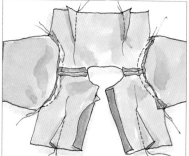

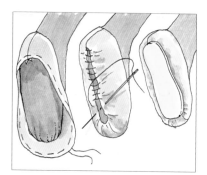

6 With right sides together, sew both front bodice pieces of the petticoat together along the neck edge, turn right side out, and press. Gather lower edge through both layers from A through B to A, then sew to petticoat skirt, clip, and press seam.

7 Sew petticoat sides together with French seams, then sew across shoulders. Turn lower edge up to front, press, and cover raw edge with lace. There is no need to finish armholes or back neck edge since the petticoat remains out of sight and will not be removable. Stuffing can be placed in petticoat bodice to provide additional bust shaping.

8 Sew side seams of skirt, hem lower edge, and gather waist. Before pulling up put it on doll, pull up gathers, arrange fullness, and sew to body beneath.

9 Make darts on front and back dress bodice and sew together at shoulders. Gather each sleeve cap (head) and sew in place. Sew across facing of bodice fronts, clip corner, and trim point before turning right side out and pressing. Hem wrist edges, then sew underarm and side seams.

10 Turn under a narrow hem around the neck, then shape and arrange the lace motif into a collar and sew in place. Sew buttons to right front and put bodice on doll. The bodice can be gathered and stitched over the skirt to make a dress, or hemmed and used as a jacket. Stitch front edges together.

11 Sew heels of slippers, then run a gathering thread around lower edge, put on feet, and pull up gathers for slippers to fit snugly. Cover cardboard soles with leather and glue or stitch in place. Trim top edge of slippers with the pipecleaners glued in place to simulate a fur roll.

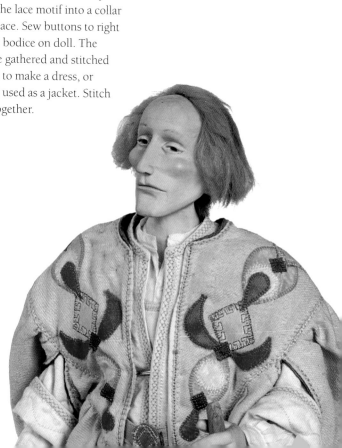

Prospero, by Julia Hills, has a cloth body and head, and hands made of air-drying clays; several different kinds mixed together to give the right color.

Santa Claus

THIS DOLL COMBINES A SCULPTURED HEAD AND LIMBS WITH A CLOTH BODY AND ARMATURE THAT MAKES A FULLY POSEABLE CHARACTER STANDING 17 IN (43CM) TALL. IT ALSO PROVIDES A WONDERFUL OPPORTUNITY FOR CREATIVITY SINCE IMAGINATIVE USE OF DIFFERENT MATERIALS, COLORS, AND HAIR STYLES WILL LEAD TO ADDITIONAL CHARACTERS.

MATERIALS NEEDED FOR THE DOLL

Modeled head with adult features, pair of lower arms, and boot legs

13 x 18 in (33 x 46cm) curtain lining

7 oz (200g) stuffing

7 in (18cm) white crepe hair

Clear all-purpose glue

55 in (1.4m) aluminum armature wire

Epoxy putty or quick-setting plaster

Dental floss or strong thread

Styrofoam pellets (polystyrene chips)

Electrical insulation tape

MATERIALS NEEDED FOR THE CLOTHES

24 x 45 in (61 x 115cm) red velour

18 in (46cm) square of white fur fabric with ½ in (12mm) pile

12 in (30.5cm) narrow elastic

3 snap fasteners (press studs)

Fabric of your choice for sack

Cord for sack

MAKING THE DOLL

1 **(Above)** The head, hands, and boots needed to make Santa Claus should all be approximately 3 in (7.5cm) long, and the head should have a circumference of 10 in (25cm). You can sculpt your own from clay or use porcelain parts taken from a kit as shown here.

2 **(Below)** Fold each arm and leg in half with right sides together and sew each in turn from A to B. Leave inside out. Sew body pieces together down each side from C to D. Again leave inside out.

3 **(Below)** Place shoulder plate sections right sides together and sew from E through F–G–G–F to E on other side. Trim curved seams, especially the neck, rather than clipping. Turn right side out, press, and stitch opening to close.

4 Cut armature wires for body: two x 15 in (38cm) for the legs and two x 10 in (25cm) for the arms. Half-fill each porcelain limb with pellets (chips). Then push in matching wires and set with either plaster or epoxy putty (page 24). Mark CB of each leg on the porcelain rim with pencil, and label the inside center (palm) of each arm in the same way. Cut a length of dental floss, and starting at B with a knot and a backstitch, gather the groove line of a fabric leg piece. Leave thread hanging. Repeat with second leg and both arms.

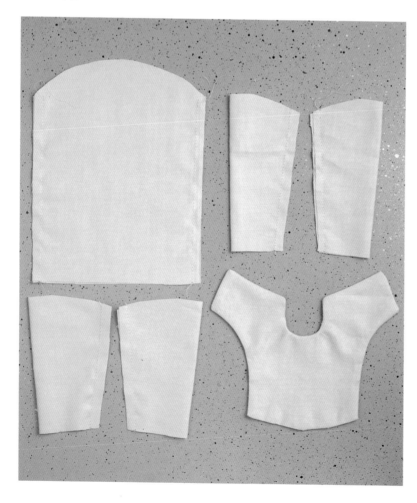

5 Run glue into the groove on the porcelain leg, then feed into fabric leg lining up pencil mark with seam at CB. Pull thread up tightly. It will sink into groove. Distribute gathers evenly, wrap thread around groove, and fasten off at seam. Finish all limbs in the same way and leave to dry overnight.

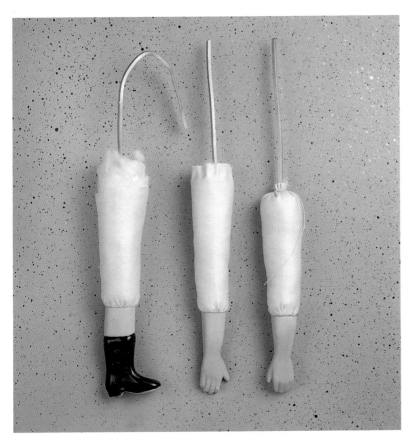

9 Bring leg wires together and bind with insulation tape. Place arm against body with thumb facing forward and seams together, and pin in place. Lift arm at a right angle to body and where wire meets leg wires—approximately 2 in (5cm)—fold up, and bind wires together.

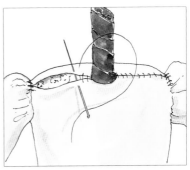

10 Secure second arm to body in the same way, binding wire to the central column. Now use threads hanging from arms to sew them in turn to the side seams, enclosing raw edges inside body. Close shoulder seam, oversewing front to back on each side of wires. Add more stuffing as necessary to make a really firm body.

6 Pull fabric leg upward and stuff firmly to within ½ in (12mm) of the top. Make sure the wire is central, surrounded by stuffing as bone is to muscle. Repeat for second leg and arms, but stuff arms less firmly. Run a gathering thread along each shoulder line in turn, then pull up tightly, wrapping thread around wire several times before fastening off, leaving thread hanging.

7 Slide a rubber band through an empty spool (cotton reel) and position between legs, slipping a loop of rubber over each foot, checking that right and left feet are correctly placed. This supports the leg and prevents the porcelain from breaking. Now position body over legs so the shoulder opening is at the toe end and the base is level with the tops of the legs.

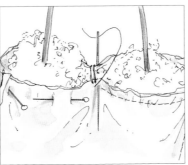

8 Pin, then sew with a small running stitch from D to H on the back of each leg, around front, and back to D. Take several stitches through all layers at H to create a crotch before fastening off. Pull up body and stuff firmly to the shoulder.

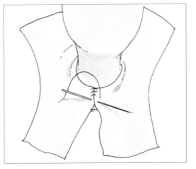

11 Wrap shoulder plate around neck, bringing Gs together. Overcast CB seam from G to F. The head should fit snugly but still be able to rotate. Place head on body over wires and pin in position. Check tilt of head before sewing.

MAKING THE HAIR AND BEARD

These features are described here, but you can if you wish wait until after Santa has been dressed to make them, as the costume will determine how the hair falls, how much you may need to use, and what alterations might be needed.

12 Pull hair from the braid, teasing fibers apart until there is enough length to cut two batches of 2 in (5cm) crinkle. Split both batches in half, making four equal-sized fringes, one for each row of hair.

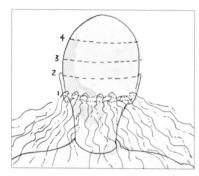

13 Run a line of glue along Row 1, which is the hairline between the ears. Take one fringe, tease it out further to fit, then press ends firmly into glue and leave to dry. Glue a fringe in place on Row 2, which is level with top of ears, and then Rows 3 and 4, which extend from the temples on each side, leaving a bald patch on top.

14 Prepare hair for beard by pulling and teasing out more fiber from the braid, cutting two batches of 2½ in (6.3cm) crinkle. Take first batch of crinkle and split off two thirds to start the beard on Row 1, keeping the remaining third for the sideburns. Put a line of glue under jawline between ears and spread hair to fit before gluing in place. Hair will stick up, but it can be stroked down when glue is dry.

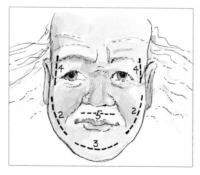

15 Take second batch of crinkle and split in half. One half is used for Row 2 and the other half is for Rows 3 and 5. Using the hair for Row 2, divide equally, teasing out each fringe to fit from ear to corner of mouth. Glue each side in place. Now, using the remaining half, pull off enough for a small fringe on chin at Row 3 and glue in place.

16 Divide fringe for sideburns in half and glue at Row 4 so they hug the side of the face. Now take remaining piece of fringe from second batch of crinkle and twist in the middle to make the mustache. Glue in position, with the twist firmly pressed into the glue beneath the nostrils at Row 5.

17 Take tiny pieces of hair from that remaining on the braid and glue to each eyebrow. Use rest of hair as you please to make a fine covering for the top of the head. Trim and groom both hair and beard after patting into place.

MAKING THE CLOTHES

When working with velour, it is advisable to finish all raw edges as you complete seams and to fold back single layered hems and facing. This can be done either by overcasting by hand or a machine zigzag stitch.

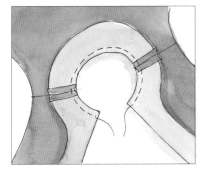

18 **JACKET** With right sides together, sew jacket fronts to back on each shoulder from A to B. Complete neck facing by sewing back facing to front facing along D–E on each side, then fold, bringing neck edges together and sew facing to jacket from CF through A–C–B–A to CF on other side. Trim corners, clip curve, and turn facing right side out.

19 Position each sleeve in turn, matching C–B–Cs, and sew shoulder seam, then each underarm and side seam from F through C to G. Turn up a hem and sew a small running stitch, 1 in (25mm) from the folded edge. Then do the same with the sleeves and front facings. These rows of stitches act as a guide for placing fur trims.

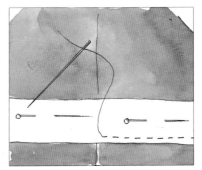

20 Take one of the three strips of fur and place the lower edge right side down across the bottom of the jacket along the stitching line just made. Sew fur to jacket with red thread, 1¼ in (32mm) from folded edge. Now turn fur downward and, with white thread, ladder stitch to jacket as close to the edge as possible. Pin center front trim to right jacket front and attach in the same way.

21 Take second strip of fur and cut in half, one for each sleeve. Attach in the same way, but start at the seam and work around the sleeve back to the seam. Trim off any excess fur, butt the edges, and overcast together. Turn down and ladder stitch to the folded edge.

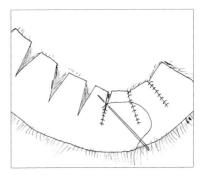

22 Shape the collar by butting the edges of each dart together and overcasting. This will fold the collar around. Place against neck, right side uppermost, with ¼ in (6mm) protruding above neck edge. Ladder stitch lower edge of collar to jacket, then turn under protruding neck edge and sew down. Finish jacket by sewing on snaps (press studs).

23 **PANTS** Make pants by placing right sides together and sewing A to B on each side in turn. Finish seams, waist, and lower leg edges. Refold, bringing Bs together, and sew inside leg seams C–B–C. Fold down at waist with facing to the inside and sew both layers together with a running stitch ½ in (12mm) from the edge to form a casing. Leave a small opening at CB. Turn pants right side out and cut elastic to fit waist. Insert in casing, overlap ends and, sew them together.

24 Turn up leg hem to inside and work two rows of gathering. Pull up to fit leg, then fasten off. Finish second leg in same way. Now cut remaining strip of fur in half, one for each leg. Trim legs the way the sleeves were trimmed.

25 **HAT** With right sides together, sew around hat, leaving straight edge open. Finish seam and facing edge. Turn right side out and fold facing up to wrong side. Sew two rows of gathering through the folded edge and pull up to fit the head before fastening off. Take hat trim and pin it to the hat, right sides together, 2 in (5cm) from the folded edge. Sew in place like the sleeves, butting fur edges together. Then turn downward, folding fur to inside of hat and hem in place.

26 Make the pompom by drawing a 1¼ in (32mm) circle in the middle of the fur square, then remove three sides of the square by cutting diagonally on each side to make a triangle. Run a gathering thread around the circle and as it is pulled up, tuck in the wings of the triangle to self-stuff the pompom. Sew in place on the hat.

27 Finish by making a sack and filling it with gifts and toys. Remember to have some peeping out at the top to add both color and excitement.

Santa Claus wearing a striking, crazy patchwork costume trimmed with black fur.

emma

REPRODUCING PERIOD COSTUMES IN MINIATURE IS ALWAYS A CHALLENGE, AND EMMA'S SIMPLE LONG-WAISTED DRESS WITH A MERE RUFFLE FOR THE SKIRT IS NO EXCEPTION. THIS IS DRESSMAKING WITH A DIFFERENCE, AND WITH A LAVISH USE OF LACE AND A CHOICE OF HAIRSTYLE AND FOOTWEAR, YOU WILL HAVE A YOUNG GIRL OF THE 1880s FOR YOUR DOLLS' HOUSE.

MAKING THE DOLL

You will need a dolls' house doll measuring between 3¼ and 3¾ inches (8–9.5cm) tall, cloth-bodied or bisque.

Painted footwear can be left as it is or covered with leather boots, provided there are no heels to get in the way. Since dressmaking involves much handling of the doll, it is advisable to leave making the wig till the very end.

MATERIALS NEEDED FOR THE CLOTHES

4 in (10cm) tubular bandage

6 in (16cm) square of finest white cotton lawn

9 in (23cm) narrow lace to trim underwear

3 x 1 in (7.5cm x 25mm)-wide lace, net, or lightweight jersey for stockings

9 in (23cm) square of lightweight silk

9 in (23cm) square of lightweight iron-on interfacing

6 in (16cm) of pleated silk, ribbon, or lace about ½ in (12mm) wide

Selection of narrow laces, braids, and silk ribbon to trim dress

Small buttons (optional)

Scrap of thin leather for boots

Commercial edge sealer

MAKING THE UNDERWEAR

1 From tubular bandage, make a body suit to which clothes can be attached during construction. Turn one end down inside the tube to double it, then place it on the doll with folded edge at shoulders. Then catch together both sides of the neck with a few stitches. Pull raw edges down and catch together between legs.

2 Cut stocking lace in half and arrange each stocking so that the tops are level with the knees. Apply a thin line of glue along one cut edge and anchor it at center back, then trim the other edge to fit with a slight overlap before gluing it down.

3 Turn a narrow fold to the front on lower edges of bloomers and cover with lace stitched in place to hide the raw edges. Sew center front and back seams, then inside leg seams. Turn right side out and run a gathering thread around the waist. Put dress on doll, pull threads up, and fasten off.

4 Turn a narrow fold to the front on lower edge of petticoat and cover with lace as directed for the bloomers. Sew short edges together, turn right side out and run a gathering thread around the top. Put dress on doll with top either above or below top of bloomers to reduce the bulk and sew in place.

5 Cloth-bodied dolls are frequently too bulky at the waist so wind a thread tightly around the waist to pull it in. The underwear can also be pulled tight to give more shaping. A hint of a bustle can be indicated by drawing gathers of underwear to the back and adding a large bow to the dress.

MAKING THE DRESS

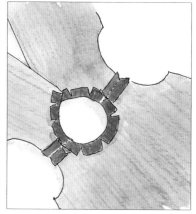

6 Sew shoulder seams and press, then fit on doll to check fit of neck. Clip the curve to get a tight fit, then turn under a narrow hem and secure with glue or tiny stitches. Sew side seams, press, and finish by turning up a narrow hem along bottom edge.

7 Use a ready-made trim for the skirt or make your own by pleating or gathering suitable lace or silk and place it behind the hem. Check length, then topstitch skirt to dress from the front by hand using small running stitches. Turn back edge under on one side only and press.

8 Glue lace on the inside to cover raw edges of skirt and hem. Using deep lace will give the impression of another petticoat without making additional bulk at the waist. Put dress on doll, overlap back edges, and glue in place to close. Decorate dress front with lace, braids, and buttons.

9 Emma's skirt has an additional lace overskirt with another narrow lace covering the top edge. Small silk bows are glued at center front and back, and two strands of embroidery thread, matching the color of the ribbons, have been woven in the heading of the lace.

10 Turn under the wrist edge of each sleeve, press, and decorate with lace to make cuffs, or leave them plain. Sew side seams, turn right side out, and run a gathering thread around each top opening. Place sleeves on arms and match cap of sleeves to shoulder seams, and underarm seam to side seam. Pin at the shoulders.

11 Pull up gathering thread, gently stroking raw edges under. When you are happy with the fit, ladder stitch in place. Try not to stitch too far out onto the dress or the bodice will pucker and the arms won't turn. Take your time and sew carefully.

"Mein Liebling"—this charming dolls' house doll was reproduced by the author and costumed by Syliva Critcher in an 1880s costume.

MAKING THE BOOTS

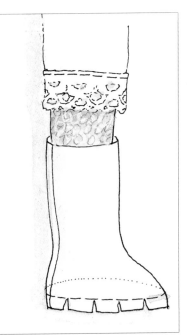

12 Fit leather against leg to determine correct size. The straight edge should reach around the leg with a small overlap and the curved edge should be long enough to turn over the edge of the foot. Trim away any excess, then glue onto leg, pulling and stretching for a good, wrinkle-free fit.

13 Either cut soles freehand or stand the doll on paper and draw around the feet to make a pattern. Glue soles in place and crease a heel mark with your fingernail. Draw on buttons and trims with fine-line pens.

cutting guides and patterns

ALL THE PATTERN PIECES FOR MAKING THE DOLLS IN THE "DOLLS TO MAKE" SECTION ARE FOUND ON THE FOLLOWING PAGES. MOST ARE PRESENTED ON "PATTERN GRIDS," WHILE REGULAR SHAPES SUCH AS RECTANGLES FOR SKIRTS AND PETTICOATS ARE GIVEN SIMPLY AS MEASUREMENTS IN THE "CUTTING GUIDES." THERE ARE TWO SIZES OF PATTERN GRIDS: GRID 1 IS MADE UP OF ¹⁹⁄₃₂ IN (15MM) SQUARES AND GRID 2 IS MADE UP OF ⁷⁄₁₆ IN (11MM) SQUARES. TO MAKE THE FULL-SIZE PATTERN PIECES, YOU WILL NEED TO ENLARGE ON A PHOTOCOPIER TO MAKE THE SQUARES MEASURE 1 IN (25MM). ALSO REFER TO THE INSTRUCTIONS GIVEN ON PAGE 18 FOR "MAKING A PATTERN."

You should note that a seam allowance of ¼ in (6mm) is included on all patterns unless otherwise stated.

The "cutting guides" for each project list which fabrics to use for each piece and will draw your attention to any special features such as stretch, nap, and advance preparation of materials. Directions for construction will generally follow the order of making paper patterns followed by cutting from relevant fabrics as directed by the cutting guide, then sewing together.

The Simple Starter Doll, Stretch Jersey and Felt Dolls, however, are made by using templates (see pages 130, 134–135) rather than patterns and the order of construction differs from that outlined above as many pieces are sewn together before the fabric is cut. In this instance you will need to make full-size card patterns without a seam allowance. These are then used as templates to draw around and thus mark the sewing line so that accurate seams can be made when sewing curves and intricate shapes. At this point the fabric is cut into separate pieces, adding the seam allowance, and construction continues.

All instructions for how to make a pattern and lay it out, and explanations of pattern markings, are on pages 18–19.

BASIC CLOTH DOLL

see Project page 95
see Pattern page 131

Make a full-size pattern of all pieces on the grid. The body front and back are almost identical. Make two copies of the back, then trim one across the lower edge to make the front.

In addition, you will need to make patterns for the following:

Panties—8 x 6 in (20 x 16cm)

Petticoat—8 x 24 in (20 x 61cm)

Skirt —8¾ x 22 in (22.5 x 56cm)

Bias strip for neck—6 x 1½ in (16cm x 36mm)

Cut body, arms, and head from muslin (calico), legs from printed cotton, and underwear from cotton lawn. Cut neck bias from a corner of the second printed cotton, then the remainder of the dress.

STRETCH JERSEY DOLL

see Project page 103
see Pattern page 134

Make a set of paper patterns. Trim away the seam allowance on all the body pieces, and glue to card, making a set of templates. Sew face, arms, and legs in jersey before cutting out. Then sew body in chosen fabric before cutting.

Trim the complete seam allowance away from the vest (waistcoat) and just the upper edge of the boots. The vest and boots are made from the same fabric. Sew each to respective lining fabric before cutting out.

In addition, you will need to make a pattern for the skirt measuring 7½ x 20 in (19 x 51cm) and a pattern for the waistband measuring 2½ x 7 in (6.3 x 18cm). Cut sleeves and waistband from matching fabric and skirt from another fabric.

FELT DOLL

see Project page 106
see Pattern page 135

Make a full-size set of patterns of all pieces on the grid. Remove the seam allowance from the arms and legs to make sewing templates. Then remove seam allowance from the center front and center back edges only, of both body pieces. Also, prepare a pattern for the shoe straps, measuring ½ x 5½ in (12mm x 14cm).

Use flesh-colored felt for the limbs, sewing them together in pairs before cutting out. Cut a piece of flesh-colored felt measuring 8 x 7 in (20 x 18cm) for the face mask. Then cut a piece of cheesecloth (butter muslin) or buckram, the same size, to line the mask.

The body is cut from muslin (calico) after the center front and center back seams have been sewn. Cut wig from fur fabric following step 9, on p.109.

Cut panties, bodice, and skirt for the dress, from the main colored felt. The back skirt has a center back slash extending down from the waist. Make a slash down the center back of the bodice from the neck so that the dress will fit onto the doll. Cut shoes and decorations for the dress from contrast felt.

SPOON DOLL

see Project page 111
see Pattern page 136

Make full-size patterns of all pieces on the grid. Join body top and skirt pieces together at the waist to make one complete pattern piece for the body/dress.

Cut body/dress, sleeves, and large oval base from fabric print. In addition, cut a ruffle from dress fabric which measures 4 x 36 in (10 x 92cm). This is used to decorate the lower edge of the dress. Cut a small card oval, for the base.

Remove seam allowance from hand and alternative head patterns. Use both as templates to sew hands and head on doubled muslin (calico) before cutting out.

BABY DOLLS: SLEEPY HEADS

see Project page 114
see Pattern page 137

Make a set of full-size pattern pieces from the grid. Cut body pieces and beanbag from the sleep suit fabric. Cut head and hands from stocking fabric with most stretch passing around the head. When you come to sculpt the hands, line the fingers up with the direction of knit stitches on the fabric.

ARMATURE DOLL: HANNAH

see Project page 116
see Pattern page 138

The body for Hannah consists of a bound and wrapped armature. The measurements and patterns given are for a doll with a head length of 2¼in (5.7cm) measured from chin to forehead. Measure your sculpture carefully, checking the size and make adjustments as necessary before cutting the wires. Make sure you alter all other pattern pieces accordingly. A slight variation in either direction—½ in (12mm)—could make a doll as much as 2 in (5cm) taller or shorter.

Cut armature wire for arms so that when they are set into the hands, the total length from fingertip to fingertip is 17 in (43cm), or just slightly less. Cut wire at 38¼ in (97cm) for the legs and body. Cut batting (wadding) into long strips, 1in (25mm).

Make full-size pattern pieces for the underwear and dress, then cut from crepe de chine and cotton print, respectively. Cut slippers from fleece, with soles from both cardboard and leather, the latter cut ⅛ in (2mm) larger all around.

Simple Starter Dolls:
Rectangular pillow doll and Triangular pillow doll

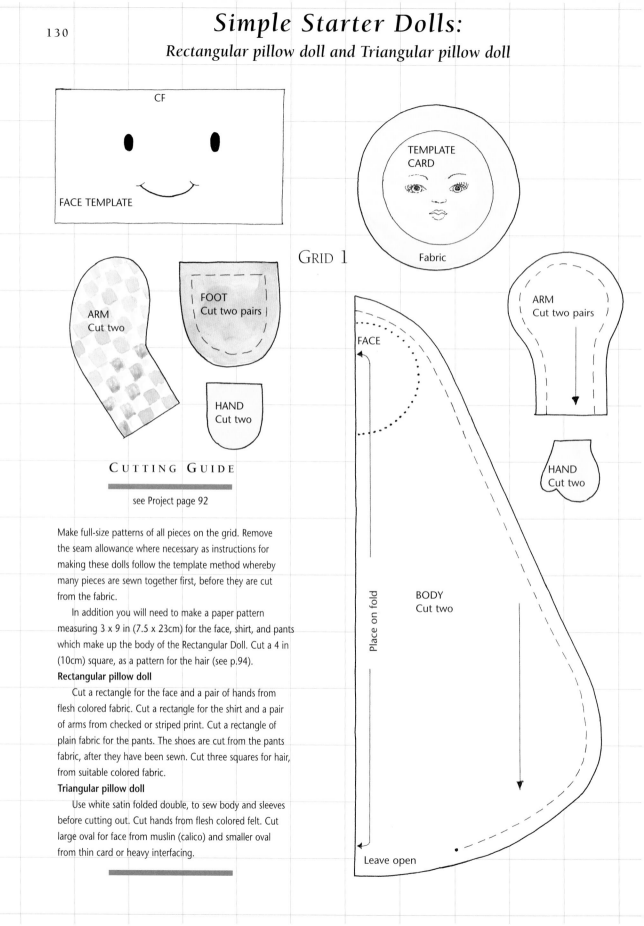

CF

FACE TEMPLATE

TEMPLATE CARD

Fabric

GRID 1

ARM
Cut two

FOOT
Cut two pairs

ARM
Cut two pairs

HAND
Cut two

FACE

HAND
Cut two

CUTTING GUIDE

see Project page 92

BODY
Cut two

Place on fold

Leave open

Make full-size patterns of all pieces on the grid. Remove the seam allowance where necessary as instructions for making these dolls follow the template method whereby many pieces are sewn together first, before they are cut from the fabric.

In addition you will need to make a paper pattern measuring 3 x 9 in (7.5 x 23cm) for the face, shirt, and pants which make up the body of the Rectangular Doll. Cut a 4 in (10cm) square, as a pattern for the hair (see p.94).

Rectangular pillow doll

Cut a rectangle for the face and a pair of hands from flesh colored fabric. Cut a rectangle for the shirt and a pair of arms from checked or striped print. Cut a rectangle of plain fabric for the pants. The shoes are cut from the pants fabric, after they have been sewn. Cut three squares for hair, from suitable colored fabric.

Triangular pillow doll

Use white satin folded double, to sew body and sleeves before cutting out. Cut hands from flesh colored felt. Cut large oval for face from muslin (calico) and smaller oval from thin card or heavy interfacing.

Basic Cloth Doll

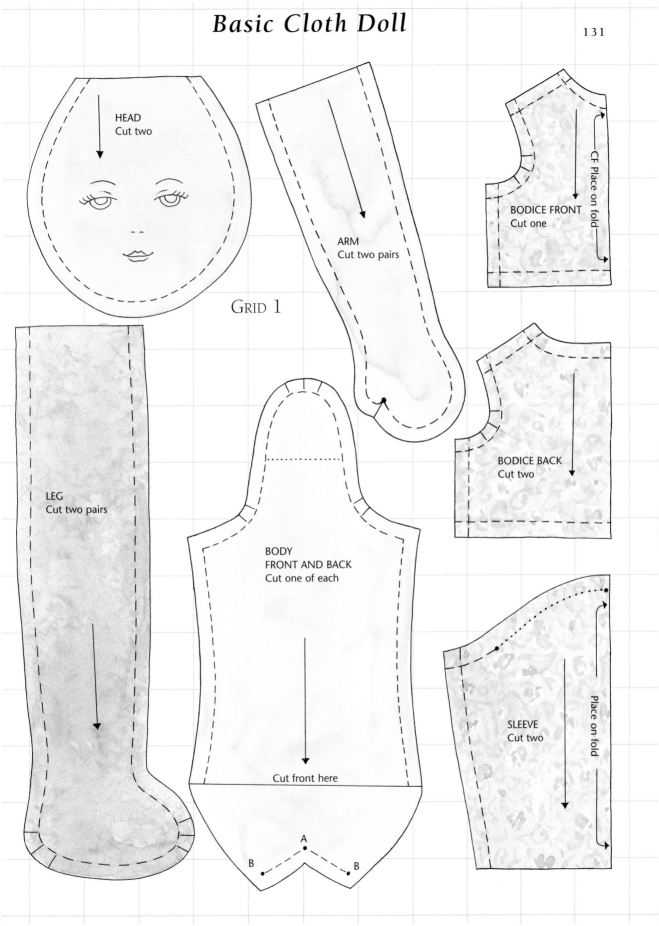

HEAD
Cut two

ARM
Cut two pairs

BODICE FRONT
Cut one

CF Place on fold

GRID 1

BODICE BACK
Cut two

LEG
Cut two pairs

BODY
FRONT AND BACK
Cut one of each

Cut front here

A

B   B

SLEEVE
Cut two

Place on fold

Crafted Cloth Doll: *Lavinia*

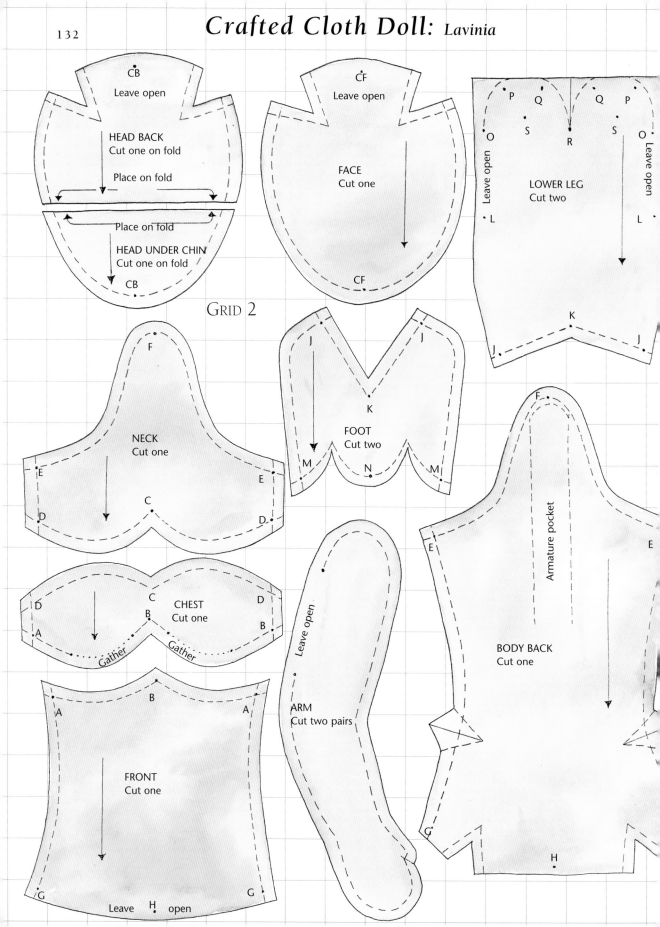

CB
Leave open

HEAD BACK
Cut one on fold

Place on fold

Place on fold

HEAD UNDER CHIN
Cut one on fold

CB

CF
Leave open

FACE
Cut one

CF

P   Q   Q   P

O   S   R   S   O

Leave open

Leave open

L   L

LOWER LEG
Cut two

K

J   J

J

GRID 2

F

NECK
Cut one

E   E

D   C   D

J   J

K

FOOT
Cut two

M   N   M

D   C   D

A   B   B

Gather   Gather

CHEST
Cut one

F

Armature pocket

BODY BACK
Cut one

E   E

B

A   A

Leave open

ARM
Cut two pairs

FRONT
Cut one

G   G

Leave   H   open

G

H

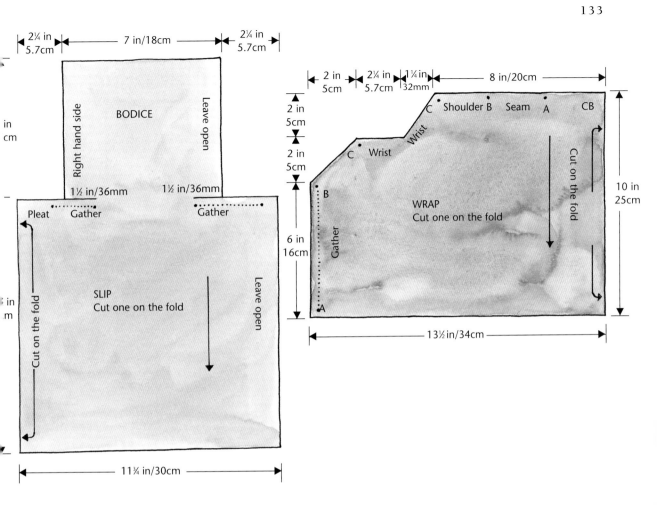

CUTTING GUIDE

see Project page 98

Cut all body pieces from muslin (calico). In addition, you will need a muslin (calico) strip measuring 1½ x 6½ in (36mm x 17cm) for the armature pocket and two pieces each measuring 5½ x 7 in (14 x 18cm) for the upper legs.

The panties are made from the pants pattern for Santa Claus. Cut a new pattern piece that has 1½ in (36mm) trimmed from the leg edge and has the waist edge extended upward by 1in (25mm). Cut two pieces from silk satin. The slip is cut from a piece of silk satin measuring 18 x 23½ in (46 x 60cm) wide. The bodice shaping and waist darts are given as measurements on the pattern diagram.

Cut the dress silk in half to make two rectangles, each measuring 10 x 22 in (25 x 56cm). Measurements for the wrap are given on the pattern diagram. Make a paper pattern, transferring the instructions, then cut from shot silk. The turban is a simple rectangle measuring 14 x 16 in (35.5 x 40cm) cut from your chosen fabric.

Stretch Jersey Doll

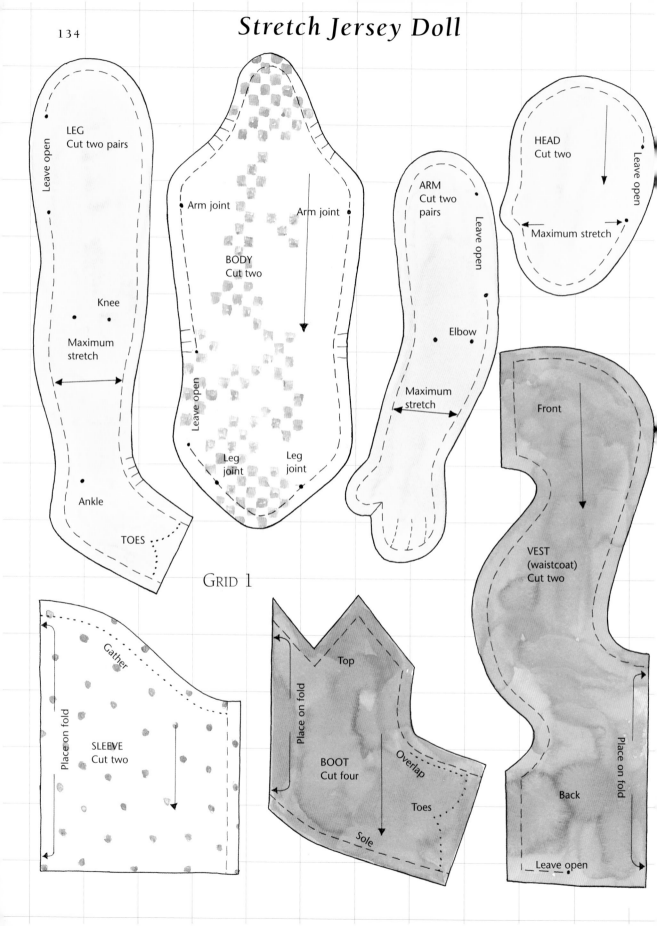

LEG
Cut two pairs

Leave open

Maximum
stretch

Knee

Ankle

TOES

BODY
Cut two

Arm joint

Arm joint

Leave open

Leg
joint

Leg
joint

GRID 1

ARM
Cut two
pairs

Leave open

Elbow

Maximum
stretch

HEAD
Cut two

Leave open

Maximum stretch

VEST
(waistcoat)
Cut two

Front

Place on fold

Back

Leave open

SLEEVE
Cut two

Gather

Place on fold

BOOT
Cut four

Top

Place on fold

Overlap

Toes

Sole

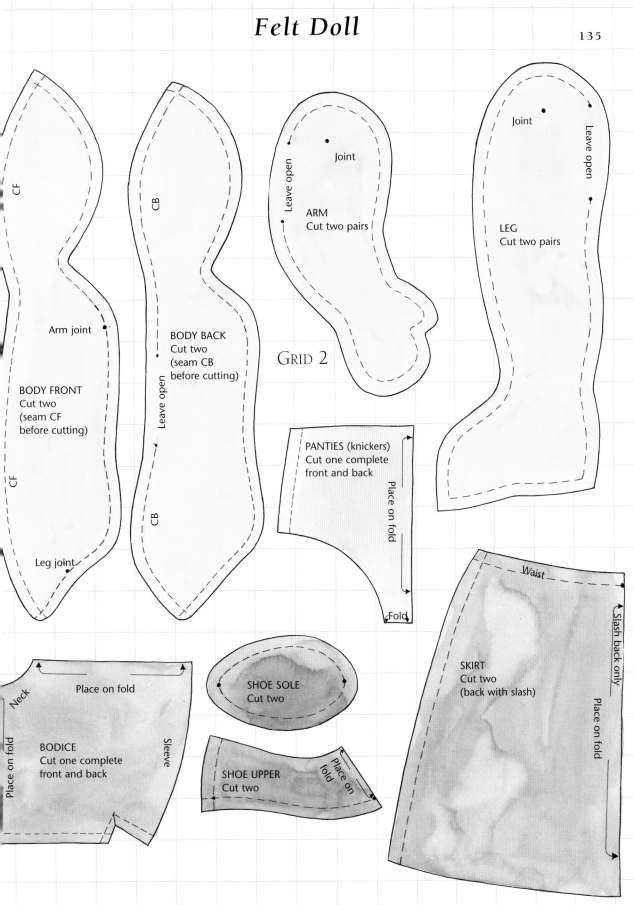

CF

CB

BODY BACK
Cut two
(seam CB
before cutting)

Arm joint

BODY FRONT
Cut two
(seam CF
before cutting)

CF

Leave open

CB

Leg joint

Leave open

Joint

ARM
Cut two pairs

GRID 2

Joint

Leave open

LEG
Cut two pairs

PANTIES (knickers)
Cut one complete
front and back

Place on fold

Fold

Waist

SKIRT
Cut two
(back with slash)

Slash back only

Place on fold

Neck

Place on fold

SHOE SOLE
Cut two

Sleeve

BODICE
Cut one complete
front and back

Place on fold

SHOE UPPER
Cut two

Place on fold

Spoon Doll

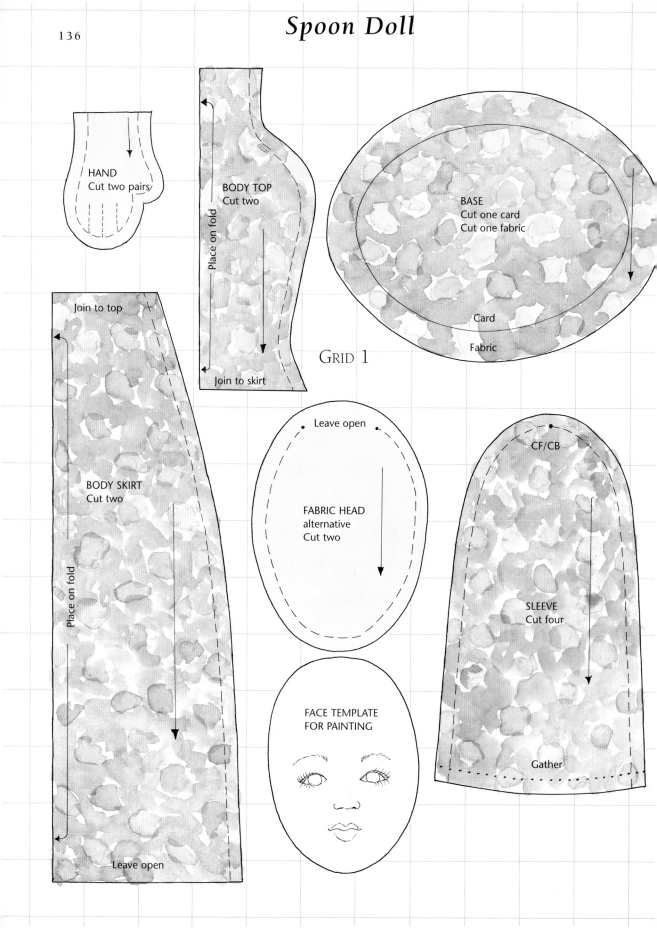

HAND
Cut two pairs

BODY TOP
Cut two

Place on fold

Join to top

Join to skirt

BASE
Cut one card
Cut one fabric

Card

Fabric

GRID 1

BODY SKIRT
Cut two

Place on fold

Leave open

Leave open

FABRIC HEAD
alternative
Cut two

CF/CB

SLEEVE
Cut four

Gather

FACE TEMPLATE
FOR PAINTING

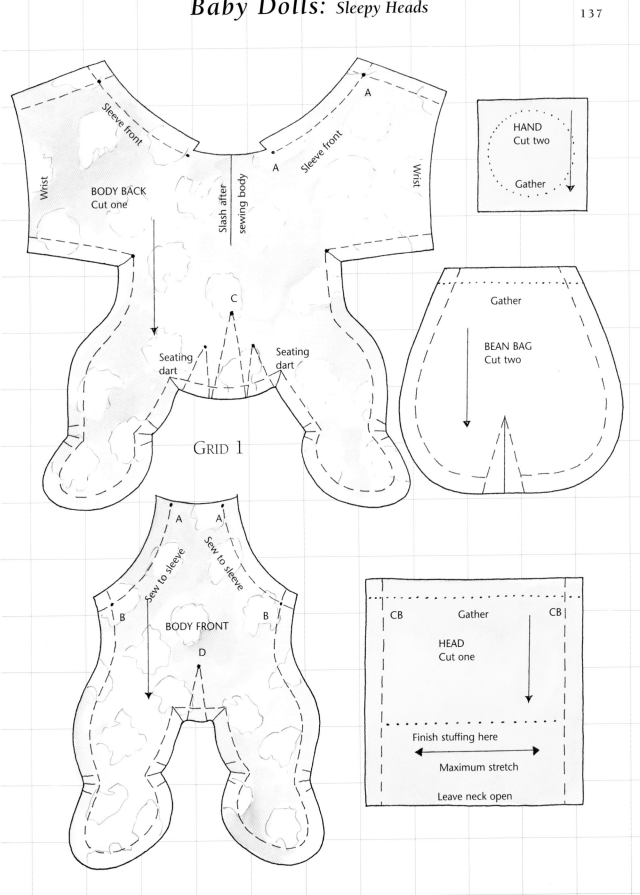

HAND
Cut two

Gather

Sleeve front

Wrist

BODY BACK
Cut one

Slash after sewing body

A

A

Sleeve front

Wrist

C

Seating dart

Seating dart

GRID 1

Gather

BEAN BAG
Cut two

A   A

Sew to sleeve

Sew to sleeve

B   B

BODY FRONT

D

CB   Gather   CB

HEAD
Cut one

Finish stuffing here

Maximum stretch

Leave neck open

Armature Doll: *Hannah*

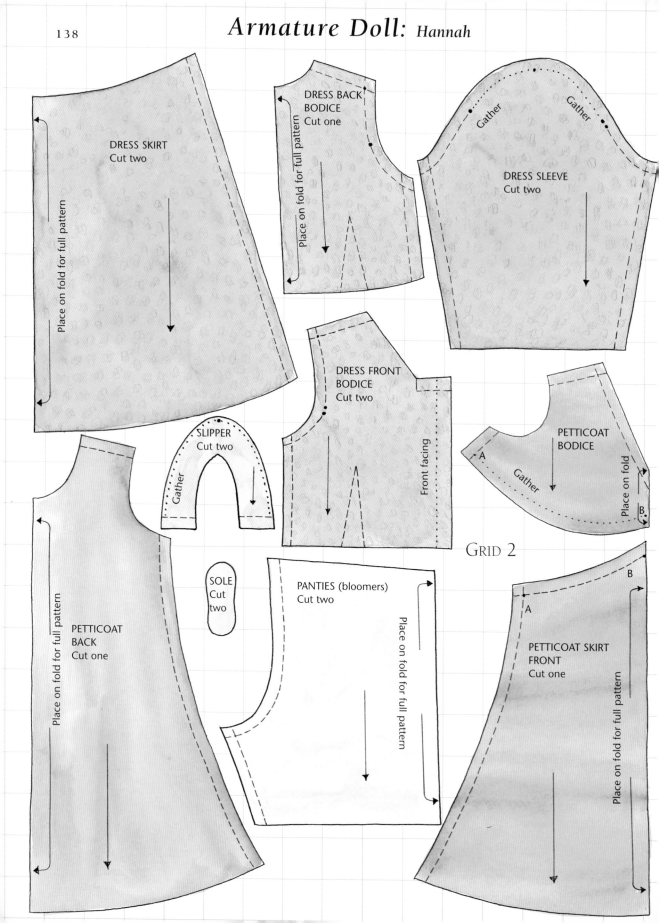

DRESS SKIRT
Cut two

Place on fold for full pattern

DRESS BACK
BODICE
Cut one

Place on fold for full pattern

DRESS SLEEVE
Cut two

Gather

Gather

DRESS FRONT
BODICE
Cut two

Front facing

SLIPPER
Cut two

Gather

PETTICOAT
BODICE

Gather

Place on fold

A

B

GRID 2

PETTICOAT
BACK
Cut one

Place on fold for full pattern

SOLE
Cut
two

PANTIES (bloomers)
Cut two

Place on fold for full pattern

A

B

PETTICOAT SKIRT
FRONT
Cut one

Place on fold for full pattern

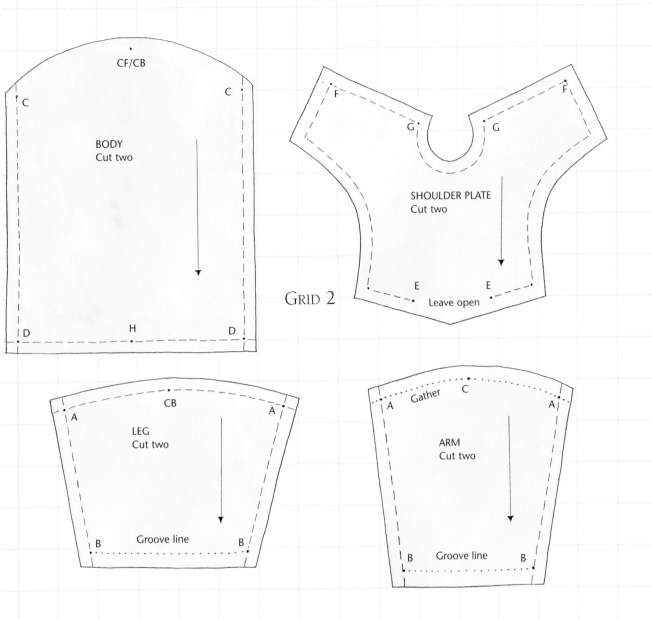

CF/CB

C   C

C

BODY
Cut two

D   H   D

F   F

G   G

SHOULDER PLATE
Cut two

GRID 2

E   E
Leave open

A   CB   A

A

LEG
Cut two

Groove line

B   B

A   Gather   C   A

A

ARM
Cut two

B   Groove line   B

CUTTING GUIDE

see Project page 119

Make full-size patterns of all pieces on graph paper. The body is cut from curtaining lining [which is heavier than muslin (calico)], while the costume is cut from velour and trimmed with fur fabric.

When cutting fur fabric, use small sharp scissors and cut through backing only. Pull fabric apart to leave pile intact. Direction of pile is downward on all garments. There is a pattern for both the collar and the center front trim, but you will need to cut additional fur trimmings for the costume as follows:

Hatband 2½ x 11 in (6.3 x 28cm)
Pompom 3 in (7.5cm) square

Cut three pieces measuring 1½ x 14 in (36mm x 35.5cm). These will be used to finish the Jacket and pant legs.

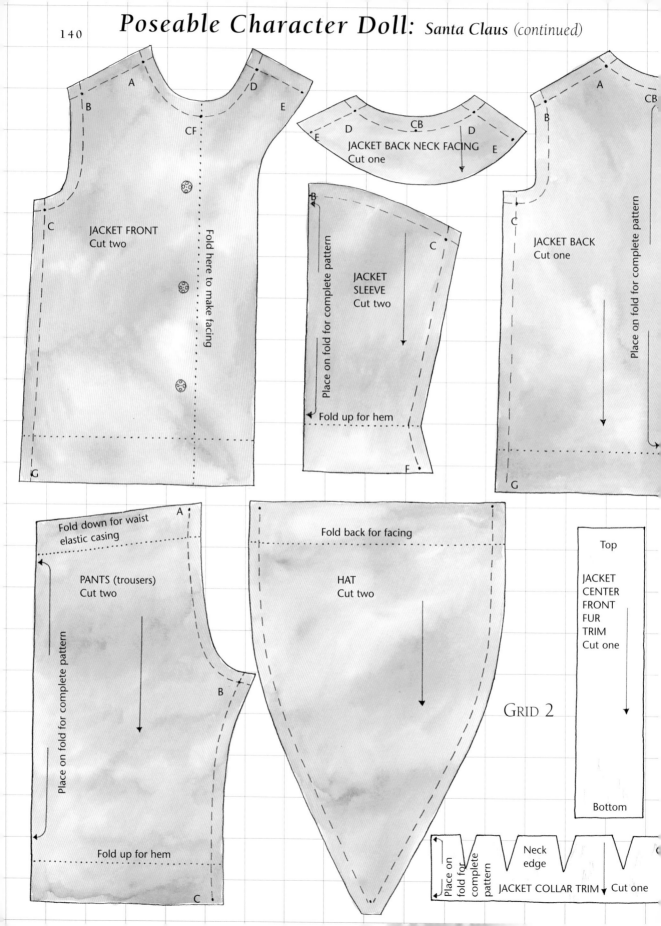

JACKET FRONT
Cut two

A
B
C
CF
G
Fold here to make facing

JACKET BACK NECK FACING
Cut one

D   CB   D
E   E

JACKET BACK
Cut one

A
CB
B
C
G
Place on fold for complete pattern

JACKET SLEEVE
Cut two

B
C
F
Place on fold for complete pattern
Fold up for hem

PANTS (trousers)
Cut two

A
B
C
Fold down for waist elastic casing
Place on fold for complete pattern
Fold up for hem

HAT
Cut two

Fold back for facing

GRID 2

JACKET CENTER FRONT FUR TRIM
Cut one

Top
Bottom

Place on fold for complete pattern

Neck edge

JACKET COLLAR TRIM   Cut one

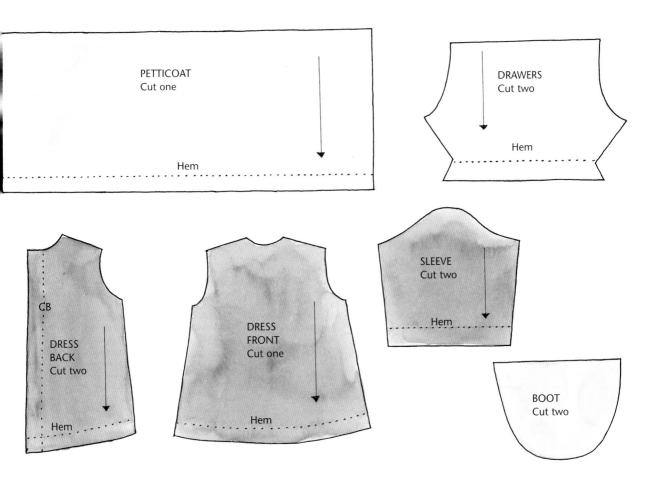

NB: PATTERN PIECES ON THIS PAGE ARE FULL-SIZE.

CUTTING GUIDE

see Project page 125

Trace full-size pattern pieces onto paper, then cut out each piece from paper towel to make a dummy pattern. Use it to fit against your doll and make adjustments as necessary for length of dress, sleeves, and width across the chest. Paper towels stretch just like fabric and can also be sewn, so they provide an excellent way of checking fit before using fabrics. Make a new paper copy of adjusted pattern pieces.

Cut underwear from fine cotton lawn, stockings from lace, and boots from leather.

Bond silk to interlining and draw around all dress pattern pieces on the interlining, but cut them out **only** as you are ready to use them.

index

As tools and techniques are illustrated on the same page as the text, illustrations are not separately noted, except for artist dolls. Captions to the latter are indicated by *italics*.

Aaron doll *71*
accessories 28–9
acetone 79, 80, 83
acrylic
    gesso 43, 74, 78, 80
    medium 40, 43
    paints 43
    varnish 40, 78
adult proportions 30–31, 98
Airman doll *60*
all-bisque dolls 35, *49, 68*
aluminum foil 65, 86
Amish dolls 35, *102*
Andrea (papier-mâché kit) *75*
anesama dolls 73
antique look 12
armatures 27, 64–7
    heads 84
    sculpting over 86–9
    see also Hannah (project);
        Santa Claus (project)
Art Deco *60*
articulation/joints 32–5
    ball-and-socket *99*
    elastic 35, 81
    manufactured 27
    wire 81
Aurora (porcelain doll) *43*

babies 30–31, 42
    see also Sleepy Heads
        (project)
backstitch 21
Baker, Susan *71*
ball-and-socket joints 33
base boards 86, 111–13
Basic Cloth Doll (project) 18,
    95–7, 129, 131
basting (tacking) seams 20
batting (wadding) 16, 17, 64
beans, plastic 16, 17
bias, working with 53
bleaching 12
blind stitching 21

bodies
    manufactured 26–7
    see also armatures
body pellets 16
braids 15
Brevette Bru doll *52*
brushes 11
buckram
    masks 61
    pates 45, 48
bullion stitch 21
buns (wigs) 49, 51
bust shaping 100
buttonhole stitch 21
buttonholes 54
buttons
    dyeing 14
    fastenings 54
    joints 34, 104
    trims 15

cabinet dolls 23
calico 12
cardboard 9, 65
carving 76
casting slips 75
Celluclay 25
ceramics, wax-dipping 42
Cernit 25
Chad Valley *60*
chain stitch 21
chalk pencils 38
chenille stems 16
China 72, 73
Chinese folk dolls *36*
Clay doll *83*
clays
    air-drying 83
    modeling (Plasticine) 24–5
    polymer 25, 29, 43, 69,
        70, 83
    water clay 86
clipping seams/corners 21
cloth armatures 65
cloth dolls
    articulation 32
    see also Basic Cloth Doll
        (project); fabrics; Lavinia
        (project); needle
    sculpture;
        stuffing

clothes
    fabrics and trims 14–15
    making 52–5
clothespin (peg) dolls 35,
    77, 79
cocktail sticks (toothpicks) 11
colors/coloring
    Amish dolls *102*
    color range 11
    faces 38–9
    flesh tones 42, 43, 78, 89
    old dolls 14
    tools 10–11
Comfort fabric 13
compasses 9
components, manufactured 26–7
composition
    joints 35
    molding 68, 71
    wax-dipping 42
cords 15
correction fluid 11, 38
cosmetics, brush-on 10, 38
Cossack (needle-sculpted doll)
    56
cotton 14
cotton balls 65
craft knives 9
crayons 10, 38
Creative Paperclay 25
crepe, theatrical 46
Critcher, Sylvia *30, 32, 49, 52, 86,
    127*
curls 23, 47, 49, 50
cutting boards 9
cutting guides 128–41
cutting lines 19

Daz 25
dolls' house dolls 14, 23
    see also Emma (project)
dough 24, 83
dowels 35, 46, 54, 65, 86, 88, 89
dressmaking 52–5
drycleaning 22
Dutch Dolls 35
dyes
    aniline 14
    commercial 12
    tea 12, 45

Effner, Diana *30, 71*
elastic
    fastenings 54
    joints 35, 81
embroidery
    combined with other
        techniques 42, 56
    hair 47
    hoops/frames 9
    Shepherd doll *85*
    see also Lavinia (project)
embroidery floss (cotton) 55
Emily (child doll) *30*
Emma (dolls' house doll project)
    125–7, *141*
English Peddler (sculpted doll)
    86
epoxy putty 24, 66
equipment, basic 8–9
excelsior stuffing 16
eyebrows 39
eyelashes 26, 89
eyes
    drawing 38–9
    manufactured 26, 41
    proportions 36
    Super Sculpey heads 87–8

fabrics
    body 12–13
    clothes 14–15
    painting 32
face masks 60–63
    manufactured 27
    molded 68
    see also Felt Doll (project)
faces
    aged 59
    appliquéd features 56
    drawing and coloring 38–9
    embroidered 42
    masks *see* face masks
    painting 43
    proportions 36–7, 84
    setting fixed eyes 41
    transfers 40
facings 54
fastenings 54
feather stitch 21
feather stuffing 16
feet 31, 85

felt 13, 63
  wigs 44
Felt Doll (project) 62, 63,
    106–10, 128, 129, 135
Fimo 25, 69, 71
fingers see hands
fixatives 29
flexicurve 9, 65
flocking 50
fly stitch 21
footwear
  boots 120, 125, 127
  shoes 29, 110
  slippers 118
forceps, surgical 9
formers 27, 65, 74
Fry Check edge sealer 9
French knots 21
French seams 53
fur fabric 62, 106, 109
fur trims 123–4
furniture 28

gathers 53, 55
gesso 43, 74, 78, 80
glitter
  crayons 38
  glues and paints 11
Glorex doll 75
Glorplast 25
glues
  craft/PVA 9, 24, 43, 60, 61,
    63, 74
  glitter 11
  safety 29
graph paper 9
Gretchen (all-bisque doll) 68
grids 18, 128
guide lines 19
gussets 33

hair see wigs
hair looms 23
Hamplemann dolls 72
hand boards 67
hands
  armatures 66–7
  proportions 31
  Super Sculpey 89
Hannah (armature doll project)
    66, 86, 116–18, 129, 138
heads
  armatures 65
  modeling 84–5
  needle-sculpting 58
  proportions 31

heirloom dolls 40
hemostats 9
Hennessey, Lorna 64, 85
herringbone stitch 21
Hilda (all-bisque doll) 49
Hills, Julia 82, 118
hinges 33
Hopi Kachinas 77

Immortals dolls 72
internal joints 34
Irebokluro (cloth-bodied doll)
    32, 44
ironing 54
  color fixing 10
  heat-bonding 12, 40

Japan 73
jars 11
J.D.K. 'Oriental' doll 48
jersey fabrics 13
joints see articulation
Jumping Jacks 72

Kami Ningyo dolls 73
Kammer and Reinhardt
    all-bisque doll 68
kapok 16
Kestner 'Oriental' doll 48
kits 26–7
knees 33, 57
knitted fabrics 13, 60
knitting needles 46
knitting yarns 22
Kruse, Kathe 60

lace 15, 125, 127
ladder stich 21
La Doll (clay) 25
Laitasalo, Ella Maija 83
latex
  casting liquid 68, 71
  paint 74
Lavinia (cloth doll project) 33,
    98–101, 132–3
layers, building-up 83
layouts 19
legs see limbs
Lenci, Madame 60
limbs 26, 57, 84–5
  see also articulation
linings 54
liquid paper 11
Lomayaktewa, Narron 77

markers, cloth 9
Massey, Maree 43
match point markings 19
Matejka, Helga 75
Matroyshkas (nesting dolls) 76
measures 8
"Mein Liebling" (dolls' house
    doll) 127
Merrett, Alicia 62
metal, wax-dipping 42
metallic glue pens 38
Milliput 24
Mod Podge sealer 40
modeling 82–5
  tools and materials 24–5
modeling clay (see Plasticine)
mohair wigs 22–3, 49
molds 68–9
  one-part plaster 70–71
  papier-mâché slip 75
  quick-impression 69
mortise-and-tenon joints 35
moss stuffing 16
mouths, drawing 39
muslin, unbleached (calico) 12

nail polish (varnish) 11, 40
  remover (see acetone)
needle sculpture 17, 56–9
  Pirate doll 102
  see also Sleepy Heads
    (project); Stretch Jersey
    Doll project)
needles
  basic types 9, 20
  for needle sculpture 57
  for painting 11
nuts, crushed 16

origami 73
oven-curing 25, 87, 89

paints/painting
  acrylics 10–11, 32
  China paint 10
  painting faces 43
  safety 29
  water-based enamels 11
palette knives 11
palettes 11
Pantin dolls 72
paper
  armatures 65
  dolls 72–3
  stuffing 16
Paper Nellas 72

papier-mâché 72–5
  casting slip 68, 71, 75
  modeling 24
  painting 43
  paste 83
  wax-dipping 42
paté de bois 82–3
pates 23, 45, 48
patterns
  doll projects 128–41
  list of markings 19
  making 9, 18
Peake, Pamela (author) 102
peddler dolls 28, 28
peg dolls 35, 77, 79
Peg Woodens 35, 76
pencil sharpeners 9
pencils
  coloring 10, 38
  drawing 9
pens
  coloring 10
  crow-quill/map 11
  fabric 38
  Micron Pigma .01: 10
period dolls 52
  authentic colors 14
  wigs 44
  see also Emma (project);
    Lavinia (project)
petroleum jelly 70, 71, 74
photocopies 40
Pillow dolls (project) 92–4, 128,
    130
pins 9
pipe cleaners 16, 65, 66
Pirate doll (needle-sculptured)
    102
pivot joints 33
plaster of Paris 41, 68, 70–71
plastic armatures 65
plastic granules 16, 17
plastic joints 34
plastic molds 68
plastic wood 24, 43, 80, 83
Plasticine 24–5, 45, 65, 83
plasticizer 29
Play doll (carved head) 76
pleats 55
polyester
  batting (wadding) 16
  fiber 16
polystyrene see Styrofoam
pompoms
  decorative 124
  stuffing 16

Pongratz, Elizabeth 76
porcelain
    casting slip 75
    dolls 10, 27, 43
poseable dolls 34, 119
    see also Santa Claus (project)
press molds 68–9
pressing 54
primers 74, 78
proportions
    bodies 30–31
    facial features 36–7
Prospero (clay-headed doll) 82, 118
Puppen Fimo 25

Queen Anne dolls 76
quilt shops 12

rag dolls 95
rag stuffing 16
reagents 29
resins 68
retardant 11
ribbons 14, 15, 54, 55
rice, plastic 16
rickrack braid 15
ringlets 23, 50
Roberts, Lesley 28, 56, 86, 102
rulers 9
running stitch 21
Russia braid 15

safety 29
    healthy stuffings 16
    heating wax 42
Sailor doll 62
sandpaper 9, 75, 78
Santa Claus (poseable character project) 28, 46, 66, 86, 119–24, 139–40
Santa, Sleepy 47
satin stitch 21
sawdust
    paste 24, 82–3
    stuffing 16
saws, junior 9
scale
    of fabrics/trims 14, 15
    pattern-making 18
scissors 8, 9
scrub sponges (grit scrubbers) 75
sculpting 86–9
    see also Hannah (project);
        Santa Claus (project)

sealing
    fabric 10, 43
    crayon color 38
    paint 11, 78
    porous surfaces 41
    transfers 40
    wood 43
seam rippers 9
seams 19, 20, 21, 53
set squares 9
sewing 20–21
sewing machines 9
Shepherd doll 64, 85
shoulder plates 84, 117, 121
silk 14, 49
Simple Starter Dolls (project) 92–4, 128, 130
skeletons 26, 27, 65
Sleepy Heads (needle-sculpture project) 114–15, 129, 137
sleeves, very small 53
smocking 55, 85
sponges 11
spoons, wooden 77, 78
Spoon Doll (project) 78, 111–13, 129, 136
stab stitch 21
stands 28, 64
steam irons 9
stem stitch 21
stitches
    for faces 42
    list of types 21
    needle sculpture 57
stockinette 13, 61, 62, 63
storage 29
straight stitch 21
stretch 12–13
    control of 57
    stuffing 17
    stretch fabric 57, 58, 60, 61
Stretch Jersey Doll (project) 59, 102–5, 128, 129, 134
strip wigs 47
stuffing 16–17
stuffing sticks 9
Styrofoam (polystyrene)
    balls 65
    chips 66
    foam 29
    head formers 27
Super Sculpey 25, 69, 86–9
Swiss tricots 13

T-shirt markers 10, 38

templates
    equipment for making 9
    for pleats 55
    for projects 128, 130, 134, 135
    for seams 20
    for wigmaking 23
textile medium 11
thimbles 9
thread spools (cotton reels) 77
threads
    basic types 8–9, 20
    decorative 21
    for ladder stitch 21
    for needle sculpture 57
    wig made of 49
tiles 11, 25
tissue paper 74
tissues 11
tools
    coloring 10–11
    modeling 24–5, 25
    wigmaking 23
    see also equipment
tracing paper 9
transfers 40
trapunto 21, 92, 94
trays, paint 11
trims 15
tucks 55
turntables 25

velours 13, 123
viscose wigs 49, 50

wallpaper paste 74
Warnes, Nyola 68
wax
    wax-dipping 42–3
    fixing eyes with 41
    molding with 71
    polishing with 75
Wellings, Norah 60, 60, 62
Whitaker, Lorna 75
wigs 22–3, 44–51
    fur fabric 106, 109
    manufactured 26
    Santa Claus
        hair and beard 122
Windsor Ponte fabric 13
wire 65, 66–7, 81
wire cutters 9
wood
    bases 28
    joints with split pins 34
    painting 43
    wax-dipping 42
    working with 76–81
wooden spoons 77, 78
    see also Spoon Doll (project)
wool
    fabric 14
    felt 13, 106
    fiber stuffing 16
    see also knitted fabrics
work stations 49
wrists 57, 66

yarn hairstyle doll 44

credits

Quarto would like to thank all the following for loaning their dolls, and who have kindly allowed us to reproduce their collection in this book:
Key: T=top B=below C=centre L=left R=right

Sylvia Critcher p.90(TR), p.119, p.124; Sylvia Critcher & Pamela Peake p.116; Narron Lomayaktewa p.5; Alicia Merrett p.91(L&R), p.92, p.103, p.106, p.111; Pamela Peake p.1(C), p.2, p.3, p.35(TR), p.36(TR), p.44(TR), p.50(BL), p.54(BR), p.72, p.73, p.90(L,TC, BC), p.95, p.97(BR), p.98, p.114, p.125; Lesley Roberts p.48(TR); Lesley Roberts & Sylvia Critcher p.28; Nyola Warnes & Pamela Peake p.55(TR).

Quarto would like to apologize if any omissions have been made.

The author would like to thank Lesley, Sylvia, and Alicia for all their help.